A Thousand Little Deaths

Growing Up Under Martial
Law in the Philippines

Vicky Pinpin-Feinstein

For Chas, Elan and Marc, whose love sustained me
while writing this book

In Memory of My Mother and Father

Photo of the author in high school in the 1970s

CONTENTS

Acknowledgements

Putting this story on paper has taken a long time. From the Washington DC suburb of Takoma Park to Sydney, Australia, where I lived for three years, and visits to other countries in between, and then back home again to Takoma, the story followed me and I followed it where it wanted to take me. It has been quite a journey.

I would like to thank Mila Tecala, who encouraged me to write. Her belief in me helped end my unhealthy view that writing was dangerous territory particularly as it related to the viciousness of the Marcos dictatorship. I express my gratitude to family members, who cheered me along the way: I am beholden to my husband, Charles Feinstein, who confidently trusted me to do right by the story. A debt of gratitude also goes to my sisters, Cynthia Daniel and Timmee Pinpin, who gave me their insights and corrected details in parts of this book. My friends in Sydney, California and in Washington have been a source of strength especially in times of hesitation and angst. You know who you are; the many conversations I had with all of you were inspirational, but more importantly, touched with warmth and humanity—that is why I am so lucky to be called your friend.

I thank my editor, Matt Ellis, who made the book what it is now and for helping me navigate the odysseys of writing. I acknowledge my gratitude to Hadley Kincade, a photo editor and graphic designer, who, after reading the book, had a remarkably clear-eyed concept for the cover, and to illustrator, Jennifer Kincade, for the chalk drawings. In February 2008, I visited the library of the Task Force Detainees of the Philippines in Quezon City. I am thankful for the access they gave me; the documents I found there have only enriched the contents of this book. I salute the difficult work they do on behalf of political prisoners.

Finally, I could not have written this book without everyone's contributions. That is not to say that everyone approves of all that is written within these pages. I take responsibility for that and for any errors despite my earnest intentions.

Vicky Pinpin-Feinstein
Washington, DC
February 2013

December 1973

"Don't stiffen your fingers. Relax them," the officer instructed me.

I was sitting on a gray metal chair next to a battered desk with him behind it. We were in a dimly lit room, furnished with worn metal office furniture. Workplaces were laid out along its walls. A strong antiseptic smell of cleaning solution pervaded the room. The odor, mixed with stale cigarette smoke, was stifling.

Men wearing khaki military uniforms sat quietly working at their desks. A few were writing by hand; others were typing on well worn typewriters with the familiar clicking sound the machines make as fingers strike the keyboard. The sound was slow and irregular, like that made by beginning typists. A few soldiers wearing camouflage fatigues sauntered into the room. After they dropped their gear onto the floor, they huddled together, talking in whispers.

I clinched my fingers, released them and clinched them again, repeating this action as if in a trance. Cigarettes smoke drifted over. I looked at the men to take my mind off the one pressing my fingertips against the paper. I heard the shrill, grating sound of opening and closing of metal file cabinets. A few men looked busy, while others seemed bored, chatting quietly while smoking away.

The man in front of me was a soldier of a military detachment unit, one of the few details I noticed as I walked into the building where a sign in big, bold black letters, 1st REGIONAL MILITARY COMMAND, CAMP OLIVAS, SAN FERNANDO, PAMPANGA was emblazoned over its entrance. The main camp, Camp Olivas, was a few miles south from where we were.

The processing area was in a small, squat gray structure that houses the military personnel working there. As the soldier continued fingerprinting me, I observed that he was of average stature for a Filipino man, around five feet five inches. Dressed in camouflaged fatigues, he had a broad face, a flat nose and dark brown Malay eyes.

"Be still," he commanded as he held my fingers uncomfortably tight. "Do not stiffen your fingers. Let me do it," he snarled.

He guided each of my fingers along the blotter, coating each one with the indigo blue ink and then one by one pressing them firmly to the form in front of him. He took his time with the task. My small ink-stained fingers ached from the pressure. *He wanted to hurt me.* He kept talking all the while, haranguing me with instructions on how to steady my fingers.

We continued in this manner. The more he talked the messier the fingerprinting became. I closed my eyes to distance myself from what was happening. I wanted so desperately to be far away from this place, to forget this was happening. *Just take me away from here,* I silently wished.

His own hands and fingers were by now heavily stained. He looked at his fingers, repelled at what he saw, and began wiping them vigorously with a sullied brown paper towel. He handed me a few of the towels to clean mine. I wiped the inky mess off to no avail. Then, it dawned on me how fitting this scene was—this image of the mess we were all in—his mess, the government's, and that of the Philippines. I was in it now too, I suppose. By staining my hands with the ink on the form that registered my fingerprints, I joined the many thousands of political prisoners under Ferdinand Marcos' dictatorship.

We were barely two hours into classes that morning. Shortly before ten, a school staff member came to the classroom with a message for the teacher. After she left, the teacher instructed me to go to the principal's office. Walking down the stairs from the third to the second floor where the office was, I felt the usual trepidation any student might feel when called to report to the principal. I was then a junior in high school at St. Scholastica's Academy, a private school founded in 1925 by German Benedictine nuns in my hometown, San Fernando. It was the same school my mother and her sisters had attended. Having been there since kindergarten, I neither found familiarity nor comfort in the office occupied by the school head, Ms. Luz Arceo, a figure dreaded by *Scholasticans*, or *Kolasas*, as we liked to call ourselves. Still, I had no hint of the trouble to come.

When I arrived at Ms. Arceo's office, I saw her talking to four men dressed in military fatigues.

"Please sit down," she told me in a firm but uncertain voice. I could tell she was not sure how to proceed. I sat, sliding meekly into the seat she offered. The soldiers remained standing. The room felt crowded. She hesitated for some time and then slowly, she spoke.

"These men are taking you with them," she announced without looking at me.

As she spoke, I noticed her voice had lost the angry tone I knew so well. Her cringing look of disapproval was also gone. When she finally looked at me, she displayed an expression I had never seen before. It was as if a new mask has been painted over her usual scowl. I knew instantly what it was: she communicated with her eyes that she neither knew what to do nor what to say. I felt her fear as it spread across her face, which was marked by a twitching and a pained expression. This was new territory for her. It was different. I immediately understood what she meant by the soldiers taking me with them.

I was by then familiar with scenes of soldiers knocking on people's doors and barging in unannounced. The Philippines had become a troubled place—chaotic, violent, militaristic, and dictatorial. For men in uniform, anything went. Men like these soldiers did not care if one was a young girl in a convent school or the leader of the underground movement. Everyone was fair game. Soldiers were ready, able, and only too willing to follow orders to arrest anyone Marcos, his cronies, and aides believed was their enemy. To them, enemies took many forms. Innocent-looking fifteen-year-old convent schoolgirls were no exception.

And then, as if on cue, my mind went blank.

The Road to Camp

It was a cool but sunny December morning as I was driven south along Highway 54, San Fernando's main thoroughfare. With the army jeep's top down, I felt the sun on my arms and face, encasing me in its warmth, a sensation vividly etched in my memory. Every now and then, a gust of wind chilled my face and then, for a moment or two, a stronger rush of wind would lift the pleated folds of my navy blue jumper uniform. I pressed the skirt against my knees in a modest gesture as I sat surrounded by men in combat fatigues.

The man in charge sat in the front seat next to the driver. He was somewhat taller than the average Filipino man, a little fairer in complexion, and young, probably in his late twenties or early thirties. He would have made a perfect poster boy for a recruitment ad—his ramrod posture allowed his uniform to fit his body precisely. He exuded cleanliness and polish, a soldier's soldier in every way.

Lieutenant Jose Bandong, Jr.—I learned his name later—was polite and respectful when he spoke with me, even if it was only to tell me to watch my step when we descended the wide concrete stairs of the school's administration building. I would not have expected this behavior from men in the Philippine military; many of them had little education. For a moment there, as we proceeded to the parking lot, I thought I detected a slight hesitation in his intent to arrest me. Yet, at the same time, I perceived an inalterable determination to accomplish the task at hand: orders were orders.

The second-in-command was a sergeant named Jose Magno; I remember his name from the badge in his uniform. I noted that both of them had the same first name. Like Lt. Bandong, Sgt. Magno was a bit taller than the two soldiers he outranked. He was also lighter in skin color. The two other soldiers were short and dark. I made a mental note of how lighter skin always increased a person's prestige in the Philippines. I was not surprised to see that the taller, lighter-skinned men also had the higher rank.

The men bowed their heads slightly when Lt. Bandong addressed them. They looked at him obediently. Their complexions and other physical features made me think they must come from another part of the country. Though they had not spoken much during the trip, my guess was confirmed when I heard them talk in Ilocano, the language spoken in the Northern Luzon provinces of Cagayan, Ilocos Norte, Ilocos Sur, and Isabela.

Kapampangans, as the natives of Pampanga are called, did not always hold a positive opinion of Ilocanos when I was growing up. It did not help that the country's president before Ferdinand Marcos, Diosdado Macapagal, the father of former President Gloria Arroyo, was from Pampanga. Many Kapampangans, at the time, believed that Marcos stole the presidency from Macapagal in what would have been the latter's second term.

I too held prejudicial beliefs regarding Ilocanos when I was young. I grew up in a status-conscious community where economic standing and social class indicated how one was treated. Coming from the "right" family name and wealth was a matter taken seriously. Going to the right school—St. Scholastica's Academy, if you are a girl, and Don Bosco Academy, if you are a boy—established your place on the status totem pole. Before my arrest, I understood little about these prejudices, and thought not to question them.

San Fernando, like many towns in the 1970s, was extremely parochial, decidedly conservative, and piously Catholic. Locals lived, worked, and had fun within the boundaries of their own community. Like many tight-knit cultures, they had an aversion to outsiders. As a young girl, I was just as class conscious as anyone around me. I was guilty in regarding dark skinned Filipinos as simply not in the same league as the Chinese/Spanish mestizo class from which my family descended. It was an unfortunate belief, considering it was now these men who had power over me. And worse, Marcos was a member of the Ilocano clan. What effect would my misguided arrogance have, when my young life was now in their hands?

Despite my terror, I shot furtive glances at the men, wanting to satisfy my last remaining bits of curiosity. *What do my captors look like?* While Lt. Bandong sat calmly in front of the jeep with one of the soldiers as his driver next to him, the two men who sat with me in the back seemed unsettled and tense. They gazed intently at the road ahead. They inhaled deeply from the cigarettes stuck between their lips; drawing on them as if these gave badly needed oxygen. They held the machine guns at their sides. No one spoke. It was as if everybody expected something bad to happen at any moment. They seemed like tigers in the wild, eager, even thrilled with the impending kill. Their vigilance was not misplaced. Ambushes were common between the military and insurgents. Pampanga has always been a hot-bed of insurgency, a cozy place for Huks[1] in the 1950s and the NPA[2] in the 1960s and 70s.

Everyone in the back seat remained on edge. My jaw, clenched tight, began to ache. As we rode along the high-way towards the military base, I saw the men finger their guns and it quickly struck terror into my pounding chest. Other than this last image, I could remember little else.

I did not know it at the time but there was another person who sat there in the back seat: my sister, Timmee, was also riding in the jeep. She filled in some of the missing details of that fateful day. This was how she related it to me some twenty years after it happened.

Ms. Arceo, though shaken by the soldiers' presence at San Fernando's most prestigious private school for girls, had had enough sense to inform my sister that there were soldiers who were about to take me away. As soon as she was told, she left quickly to go to the principal's office. The soldiers were already getting ready to leave. She saw me stand up and joined the men who were heading for the door. She followed us. Soon we were all out of the building and walked towards where the army jeep was parked.

You were all getting into the jeep and I tried to get in too, she told me. This, she said, was what happened next.

One of the soldiers stopped her and said,

"No, no, do not get in. We only came for your sister."

---

1   The word, Huk, is the moniker for insurgents commonly used in the 1950s. It is short cut for *Hukbalahap*, which stands for *Hukbong Mapagpalaya ng Bayan*, the precursor organization to the Communist Party of the Philippines.

2   NPA stands for the New People's Army, the military arm of the Communist Party of the Philippines (also known as CPP).

Timmee replied, "I have to go with her. Vicky is my younger sister. I am responsible for her."

"No, you can't go with us," the soldier insisted. As he said this, he made a threatening motion, like he was going to use the butt of his machine gun against Timmee.

It was at that point that my seventeen year old sister boldly declared, "Well, if you don't want me to go with my sister, you can just shoot me right here, but you are not going to take my sister without me."

With that, Lt. Bandong put his arms up and then rested them on the soldier's machine gun. He then commanded his men to calm down. He spoke to Timmee and told her she could come with us and wait until our parents arrived. Then we took off for the military base.

As we rode along Highway 54, I felt my innocent school-life recede farther into the distance. We must have reached the place because the next scene that I remember distinctly was the soldier taking my fingerprints. I was now at the end of the process of becoming a political prisoner. It was now mid-to-late afternoon. Timmee said she stayed at the camp for hours waiting for our parents to arrive. She called them as soon as we reached the base; she had not known before hand where the soldiers would be taking us.

My sister, Timmee, and I have always been close. She was only two years older, and there was a brother between us. Even though I love my brother, Timmee and I were closer. Yet despite our intimacy, it took us more than twenty years to finally find the courage to talk about that day. We shied away from the experience for a long time. Like me, Timmee admitted she was traumatized. But as traumatized as she must have been, she still managed to be a great sister to me. It simply never occurred to her to turn her back and walk away. I asked myself, would I have done the same thing for her? Honestly, I don't know.

We were both teenagers at the time. I was the seventh among twelve children. My older siblings always took care of me, not the other way around. I was also the youngest in the family for a long time until my mother gave birth to my sister, D., when I was six years old.

Timmee suffered from poor health when we were growing up. She had almost died twice by the time she was thirteen. She was about ten years old when, one morning, as the family sat around the table for breakfast, she collapsed and was barely caught by my father who sat next to her. She was unconscious when my parents rushed her to the hospital. Timmee related to me years later that father in his haste left the house without his shoes. She barely had a pulse and was close to dying by the time my parents reached the hospital. The doctors told them that she has a congenital heart disease, which remained undiagnosed until then. The priest was summoned to give her the final sacrament for the dying. Despite everyone's belief that she would not make it, she rallied and recovered. She had also been close to death two years prior due to a ruptured appendix. What seemed like a normal surgical procedure went terribly wrong when the anesthesiologist administered too much anesthesia, which almost killed her.

These experiences transformed her. She became more devoutly Catholic than anyone else in the family. She was determined to live and to win against the odds. Perhaps it was these experiences that taught her that she could not give up. Not even when soldiers' guns were trained upon her.

In the processing area, I was asked to complete and sign my name on forms I didn't understand nor cared to read. I felt robotic: without a body, without a soul. I could neither think nor feel anything. If I had signed my own death warrant, I would not have known it. At some point, a soldier took me inside a room to be interrogated, according to Timmee. She waited anxiously outside since they would not let her inside the room with me. She wondered when *Tatang*[3] and *Ima*[4] would arrive.

After the processing as a political prisoner was completed, the next thing I remember was of me sitting in front of the provincial commander's desk inside his office. My parents were sitting across from me. I could not hear the conversation going on. I saw my parents' lips move but I could not understand the words. I glanced at my mother who looked like she had just seen death himself. She was pale, but by turns, flustered and then angry. The more she moved her lips, the more agitated she seemed. She had difficulty keeping her composure though she sat gracefully with her legs crossed one over the other to remind me perhaps that manners were to be maintained despite the circumstances. At times she glared at me, perhaps to mask her fear. It was her way of coping, I am sure. Her eyes accused me of betrayal: *how could you do such a thing, how could you betray the family's trust, how could you drag the good family name into this?*

I turned my attention to father. He looked composed, managerial, wearing the kind of expression he must use when directing his staff at the office. There was also a tenderness that I perceived, something I rarely experienced in him. If he was fearful of what would happen to me, he did not show it. I could see him talking to the commander as if he was talking as one boss to another. He looked

---

3   *Tatang* is the Kapampangan word for father and is more formal than the shortened version of *Tang*.

4   *Ima* is Kapampangan for mother although many children shortened it by simply saying Ma.

at me calmly as if his eyes told me he understood. I was confused. *Why was Ima so angry? And how could Tatang be so calm?* It was usually the other way around. This was the father I feared, the one I never wanted to disappoint or displease. He was also the one who had much to lose professionally. My father held a relatively senior position in the government at the time, as regional director of an agency responsible for regulating small- to medium-scale industries. If this situation was not handled "properly," he could lose his job, or worse, Ferdinand Marcos would want his head. My mother was the gentle one, the one who would never pick up a fight. I expected Tatang's anger and Ima's love and understanding. Yet this, I didn't get.

Long after they left, and after I had conquered some of my fear, I remained puzzled as to why I was arrested. It was neither explained to me what charges were being brought against me nor was I informed about the laws I violated. There were thousands and thousands of Filipinos during that period whose fate was similar to mine, clueless as to why we were sent to prison and defenseless against what we endured.

Remembering

In the 1970s, San Fernando was a typical Filipino town—with its Spanish influence receding and an American influence taking its place—yet it was, to my mind, also distinctly Kapampangan.   It was Kapampangan in its proud mix of Spanish, Chinese, and Malay culinary heritage. When I was growing up, it was a modestly sized town despite being the capital of Pampanga. Even then, one could sense it was going to become a busy and prosperous place. Business was brisk; the place was growing and would attain city-status years later.

Pampanga was known for three things in the Philippines: its renowned cuisine; its Good Friday Lenten celebrations, where tourists flocked to see a living man nailed to a cross in San Fernando; and, for the huge lantern festival at Christmas time. A very old province of more than 400 years, its land mass used to include the provinces of Bataan, Tarlac, and some experts argue, even parts of Zambales. One of its towns, Bacolor, was also very briefly the capital of the country during the Revolutionary Period before the nation's independence. San Fernando's neighboring city of Angeles was also then home to the largest American military installation outside the United States, Clark Air Force Base.

At the same time that Kapampangans were intensely devoted to their Catholic faith; they also tried to combine their cultural practices with a penchant for things American. This was not difficult to do in San Fernando. Being less than a half hour away from Clark Air Force Base in Angeles, they saw American GIs on a regular basis. Many Kapampangans were also employed at Clark and could shop at its commissary. They ate American chocolates and candies, smoked Marlboro cigarettes, and watched an endless stream of American programs on their TV screens. Moreover, Hollywood movies showed one after the other at the Estrella and Frida movie theaters and then at the Miranda and Edros movie houses downtown.

For sure, anti-imperialist sentiments were growing, with America as its central target, but still in the minds of Kapampangans, America remained the enduring symbol of success. When you talked American, people listened. When you ate American chocolates and candies, in a small way, you showed how 'American' you were. For us, the word, 'American' did not merely refer to the people. The word had come to denote something to strive for, an argot for everything that was enticing and in good taste. Like our Roman Catholic faith, we became devotees of Americanism, whether it was pop music, dance, fashion, or Hollywood movies. My generation copied everything that was American. When you did, there was no question you were part of the in-crowd. You were someone with expensive Western tastes, you were not '*bana*,'[5] and a

---

5   This was a colloquial word commonly used when I was a teenager to refer to something that is lowbrow and not classy.

word conjured up by the *colegialas*[6] at St. Scholastica's and by the boys at Don Bosco, to describe the ordinary folks, particularly those below them in social or economic status. The two national cultures existed side by side and growing up in San Fernando frequently meant living in both.

This was an era of long-haired young men and mini-skirted young women in America, so we copied that style. We wore bell-bottomed pants and psychedelic-designed and colorfully patterned shirts and blouses, never mind that this was also a time of weak economy. Many would skimp on food just so they could parade down the streets dressed in fashionable outfits. We also gave free love in Europe and America a lot of attention, even though we knew that it would be frowned upon in a town that had not completely shed its straight-laced, pre-Vatican II Catholic piety. We blasted our radios to listen to American pop music that blared from the local airwaves. We considered ourselves too sophisticated for local Filipino rock, a genre of music we sneeringly believe only interested the die-hard fans of popular movie star, Nora Aunor, many of whom belonged to the working class or the poor. The Scholasticans and the Bosconians of the town's exclusive private schools would simply not have anything to do with this low-class culture.

Hippies, marijuana, the oil crisis of 1973, Kissinger and Nixon in China, the strongman Gaddafi in Libya, the butcher Idi Amin in Uganda, the military juntas in Chile and Argentina were some of the international events that were prominently covered by the Philippine press, but for some of us, we were more attuned to local happenings and were concerned that our own backyard was burning. This

---

6   A colegiala is one who attends a private school, often a single-sex school that is run by Catholic nuns.

was a time of intense student activism, one when I heard from my sister, C., who was then a student at the University of the Philippines, talked about study groups, clandestine lectures, and sit-ins organized by student activists and classes that were continually disrupted because of the demonstrations. It was a common occurrence for Ima and Tatang to drive to Manila to pick her up to protect her from the uproar and disturbances of the halls and avenues of UP and other city colleges and universities. Labor strikes, farmer demonstrations, land-grabbing politicians, Molotov cocktails, and the riot police were images I saw frequently on the news. It was also the time of the catastrophic floods that paralyzed Central Luzon in 1972.

This was also an era when those who demonstrated on the streets looked upon the rich and the prominent in the town with suspicion. I often heard the word, '*burgis*,' the Filipinized version of bourgeoisie. If you were one of the burgis, you would have to prove that you understood the plight of the masses. Even the elite, who talked about it in the same way they discussed the latest fashion, hairstyle, or the trendiest club, uttered it frequently in those days. The word was bandied about as if it was the latest battle cry. The good news was that even those in the political and economic center began to be concerned about what was happening to the country. The bad news was that it would be unusual for those in the center to fully comprehend the conditions under which the overwhelming majority lived.

It would not be an understatement to say that violence in the political arena started much earlier than the student activism. At least, that was the case in San Fernando where politically motivated murders have become common by the late 1960s. Guns were often used to settle political scores. And they have always frightened me. As a child and before I turned eleven, I lived through a violent period when San Fernando became a nesting ground for politicians' private armies and their petty conflicts. Local politicians were murdered so often that for periods at a time we were left without a mayor or other local council leaders. Gunshots were heard regularly when dusk settled across town in San Fernando's version of the Wild West. Later, the NPA joined in the tumultuous fracas with their own killing squads that rivaled those of the government. Rebels, though many did not know it, were a constant presence in San Fernando. As their numbers increased, they spread throughout Pampanga and beyond.

As children, we quickly learned not to talk about what was happening. When we played outside, we were instructed to return home as soon as it became dark. Soon after we closed our doors, we would hear gunshots ringing through the darkness across the rice fields behind the public school that was across the street from our house. The next day, neighbors would pass along the news of who had been killed or who had disappeared.

In particular, I remember one mayor we had in the late 1960s. His name was Levi Panlilio. He was a popular, decent fellow whose family we knew rather well. My grandma, *Lola*[7] Palu, or *Apu*,[8] as we commonly call her, was very good friends with his wife.

---

7   Lola is the honorific Tagalog word for grandmother. As a sign of respect, the word should be used before the grandmother's name.

8   Apu is the Kapampangan equivalent of Lola. Filipino children interchangeably use Apu or Lola.

One morning, my cousin, *Koyang* [9] N., came barging into grandma's mahogany-paneled living room as my mother's sister, *Imang*[10] Dandy, Apu, and some other cousins and siblings, were getting ready for *segundo*, the traditional mid-morning snack. My cousin could barely contain his distress. With his eyes that widened with the telling, he announced,

"I just heard in the *palenque*[11] that Mayor Panlilio was taken away last night and that he might have been killed."

"*Hesusmaryosep,*"[12] Grandma exclaimed, clutching her hands to her heart. "How do you know? When did it happen?" she asked.

My cousin said he did not know the details, he had just heard passengers on his way to town talking about it. He went on to say he heard people discussing the mayor again when he was at his mother's shop.

Days later, they found Levi Panlilio's tortured body. Apu Pa shared the grief of his widow as if it was her own. We all mourned the loss of a dear friend who had been like family, particularly to Grandma. How this could happen to such a good man was on everyone's mind.

Mrs. Panlilio's grief seemed endless. Not entirely sure how to comfort her friend, Apu Pa suggested that a vacation to the summer capital of Baguio would do her

---

9   Similar to the honorific word, Apu, *Koya* is the Kapampangan honorific word for big or older brother, cousin or close male relative. To address someone older than you, one uses the word *Koya* +ng before the person's name as a sign of respect. For an older female relative, the appropriate honorific is *atche* +ng and then the person's given name. So, were I address an older sister, I must put *atche* + ing, dropping the e and then her name, e.g., Atching Cynthia.

10   *Imang* is the honorific for an aunt or to any older female relative or nearby neighbor to show a sign of respect.

11   *Palenque* refers to the town square and its surrounding area.

12   This is a Kapampangan expression of dismay and shock, invoking the biblical names of Jesus, Mary and Joseph in a moment of fear or apprehension.

good. As plans for the trip were underway, Apu Pa asked me if I would join them. She said I could be a playmate to the widow's youngest daughter, who was my junior by two years. I was excited to go, since I had never been to Baguio and it was a summer when I had little else to do. It was my chance for a big trip away from the only place I had ever known.

The sight of the widow's grief-stricken face and her daily shedding of tears quickly dashed any notion of a happy, fun-filled trip. I thought she would never stop crying; she did so at all hours of the day and night. I was sad to see it and was perplexed that anyone could be so anguished. I had not seen that kind of crushing sorrow until then. The year was 1968 and I was ten years old.

The political violence that plagued San Fernando in the 1960s continued on to the next decade and it soon spread to other parts of the country. In the end, greed, corruption, military murders, and crony capitalism from those with political power and the violence and the lack of transparency from the underground movement were all that would irrevocably define this period in the country's history. While Marcos and his men exercised barbarism and perpetuated corruption with impunity, the Maoist-influenced NPA came up with their own distinct method of assassination, carried out by the euphemistically named "Sparrow Units." An extended period of insurgency by the left and the attacks of orchestrated mayhem and atrocity by the right gradually devolved into a wild and deadly game between the two. This impinged on the daily lives of Kapampangans and Filipinos in the rest of the country. Civilians were caught in the middle and eventually many chose to, or were forced, to take sides. So, it became a time when, you knew—though it was considered unwise to voice this—which side you were on. This was increasingly the case for many of the town's residents except for many of the girls at my school.

While all this was going on in the world around me, there were also the things that were going on inside my teenage head. I did not recognize it then, of course, but like any normal teen, I was going through the angst and confusion of my age. I did not heed these feelings as my attention was more focused on exploring the nascent stirrings of social injustice around me. At least that was what I thought. Yet, I would be lying if I said that teenage preoccupations did not bother me. Once I listened to my discontent, angst, anger, and frustration, I had become, without a doubt, a very confused and angry teenager. From time to time, the nuns at St. Scholastica's Academy suppressed my disquiet. I still followed the rules and acquiesced to the discipline imposed by the German nuns at school, but little did they really know of the turmoil inside my head. Had I told them, I imagine their advice would have been simply to pray and to keep praying.

Like many adolescents, I questioned if I had any real friends at school. It was a time of lonely walks in an emotional desert, with me often feeling like an inconsequential, small and invisible bug. It became painfully clear that I was different, very different from everyone around me. That was at least how it felt. I did not belong. I thought differently from the herd. In the dry, sandy desert that was my school, I talked about different things than the other schoolgirls. I rejected my school-mates' 'frivolities.' And for their part, I was deemed too serious. When they girlishly giggled and gossiped about teenage crushes and stylish hairdos, I felt like an outsider. I found it frustrating that they were only interested in who they were going to go to the movies with on the weekend. My sympathies were clearly with the disenfranchised, while the girls at my school worried about the dresses they would wear at the weekend parties. Or maybe the huge crushes they bestowed upon the high school boys at Don Bosco Academy. I was annoyed at their complacence and their nauseatingly positive view of the world.

How, I thought, did one even begin to think that ours was a safe and happy community? I was puzzled as to why these girls could not focus on more serious stuff. Why didn't they care that the town we lived in was becoming a violent and unjust place? Why did our society favor those who already had the means and the power, and then left the disadvantaged on the periphery? Why did they call themselves good Catholics if they allowed the poor to suffer? As I wondered about these issues, I also began to question my Catholic faith for the first time. I was beginning to feel disgruntled with what I saw as the Catholic Church's predilection for rituals rather than making concerted attempts to keep pace with the social conditions of our times. It would be a few more years until I learned liberation theology from the Jesuits.

I wished that my schoolmates took sides, and in my own selfish thinking, I wanted them on the side of those burdened by society's injustices. I reasoned that the lines were already drawn. If you and your social class identified with the powerful, with those who had the control of the country's resources, either economic or political, then you were naturally against the other side. If you identified with the disadvantaged, the countless masses, then you saw those in power as the enemy. As a teenager, I still viewed things in black and white. There was to be no shifting between the powerful and the powerless. To change sides was an unthinkable deed. You should never jump a picket line, nor should you regard Marcos as a good leader. To me, there was no such thing as 'staying neutral,' especially when blood had already been spilled. The stakes were simply too high. To keep neutral was to stay asleep, to sleepwalk through life, and that was unacceptable. I aligned myself with the activist zeal embodied by historian, activist and author, Howard Zinn, who titled his memoir, *You Can't Be Neutral on a Moving Train*.[13] That was what I thought. In my own teenage arrogance, I regarded as naïve, or worse, stupid, the colegialas in my school who thought it best to keep quiet. At the time, I was too angry to care. I justified my anger as nothing personal but something that everyone should express for the sake of the country and the mess it was in.

---

13   Aside from this being the title of his memoir, it is also the title of a documentary film of his life and times as narrated by actor, Matt Damon.

In the Shadows

"Here are two cots," announced the guard on duty as he ushered me and another young woman into the Commander's office. Due to lack of space, the room would be my sleeping quarters for the rest of my incarceration. The other young woman was about 20 years old. She was also pregnant.

"Did you tell your family to bring bedclothes for you?" the guard asked.

I nodded while the young woman replied; "My husband will be here bringing my stuff soon."

"What about food? You know, we don't feed you here. It is up to your family to supply you with your meals. If they can't, that's too bad," he continued. He was not interested in talking to us. He was simply giving orders.

"Mine is on its way," I said.

He left as soon as he settled the cots on the floor. I looked around the room and then out through a window. The building was a plain structure made of cinder blocks and concrete. Its exterior was painted a dirty white color but the paint was peeling off, leaving the naked gray concrete visible in places. It was one of an array of government buildings on a street in the neighborhood of Santo

Niño. Around the corner was the more imposing Capitol Building, home to the provincial government offices of Pampanga. Its sweeping entrance overlooked a park that was bordered by manicured hedges and rows of flowering perennials. At its center was an amphitheater. The rest of the structures surrounding this green space were regional offices of government agencies. In bold black letters, the building names read: Bureau of Internal Revenue, Bureau of Agriculture, Commission on Elections, as well as that of my father's office. His agency was called the National Administration of Cottage Industries Development Authority, or, for its acronym, NACIDA. My father was its regional director. His building stood directly across the street and ran perpendicular to the military camp.

It was dusk on the first day by the time the soldiers completed my interrogation. Ima and Tatang had already left. I was dispatched to a conference room where I saw several men chatting, reading, or sleeping. These men were, I discerned quickly, other political prisoners. Picked up in various towns and barrios of Central Luzon, they had been detained here for varying lengths of time. Some had arrived just a few days ago while others had been here longer. I wondered which one had been here the longest. Three men, talking in soft voices, were sitting on the chairs around a huge table. After the usual perfunctory hellos, the men went back to their conversations. A few of them were sitting on the floor with their backs leaning against the wall. I was introduced to everyone in the room by the guard, though their names hardly registered with me.

"This camp is not providing us with food, so please call your family and let them know they need to bring your meals regularly," a lanky man informed me as a cigarette dangled from his mouth. At the same time, he extended his hand and introduced himself.

"Thank you, I will," I replied.

"Gosh, you look so young. How old are you anyway?" another man curiously asked.

I told him. Everyone within hearing distance started shaking his head. I looked around me and realized I was the youngest person in the room. I was also the only female.

I didn't want to dwell on this. I excused myself, darted out of the room, and asked the soldier by the door if I could use the phone to call home. When I did, Tang answered. He and Ima had just arrived at the house. I told him what I needed.

"Oh, don't worry, I already thought of that. Besides, I would not want you to eat whatever they offer you there. Don't eat anything anyone offers you," he cautioned.

"Cesar is on his way. We called Aling before we left the base and instructed her to cook dinner for you. Your mother also gave Cesar a bag of your clothes, bed linens, and other things you might need. When you see Cesar, let him know what you would like to eat so Aling will cook it whenever you want," he continued.

Cesar was our family driver, and had been with us for many years so that he was treated like family. He came to us as a young man from Leyte, a province in the Visayas. Sometime later, he brought in his cousin, Aling, to help my mother keep house and cook. Ima insisted that Aling use only the recipes that she had taught her when she first came. She was picky about eating only Kapampangan dishes, not the ones Aling grew up with in Leyte.

Two soldiers arrived at the camp a short time later, escorting the pregnant young woman into the conference room. She looked tired as she waddled into the room.

Before we were introduced, I was instructed by another guard to accompany him to the lobby. Arriving there, I found Cesar, who then handed me a small suitcase and a basket of food. Soon, other family members appeared, all bringing provisions. This would become a daily ritual. Cesar would come twice daily, arriving just before lunch, and then he would come again in the late afternoon, delivering dinner and breakfast for the next morning.

Later, when everyone's food had been delivered, it was laid out on the conference table. The ones who were there earlier invited all the others to join in and to share their meals. We all sat down to eat. I picked at the food on my plate.

"What's the matter? Not hungry?" one of the men asked me.

"No, not really," I said. "Please go ahead. Take what you want." He took the bowl of food I offered and started passing it around the table. I handed him the other bowls Cesar had brought. He passed those around too. All the men ate hungrily and seemed to be having a good time. *How could they even eat?*

We sat in companionable silence, and then, after a few minutes, people began chatting. Eating was mostly a forgettable experience that first night, while talking seemed like a perfunctory attempt at being polite. Still, I was grateful that I was not eating alone in a prison cell. The pregnant young woman was at the far edge of the table from where I sat. I couldn't hear her when she mentioned her name. She seemed relaxed, eating heartily, and chatting with the men next to her. I, on the other hand, felt exhausted, giddy and somewhat shaky.

After dinner, the guard came in and told the young woman and me to follow him. He led us into the commander's office.

"Hi, I'm Annabel," the young woman said.

"I'm Vicky," I said, shaking her proffered hand.

"When did you get here?" she asked.

"I really don't remember, but it was sometime today. It's been a long day. What about you?"

"They came to my mom's store in the afternoon but I wasn't there. They waited for two hours until I arrived. Then they drove me here. I told them I wanted my husband to accompany me but they said there was no time to waste. It was almost dark when we got here. The commander had already gone home and they said I would have to wait until tomorrow to be interrogated," she explained.

"Oh," I said. I did not know what else to say. *How do I tell someone that I couldn't remember what I had gone through just hours ago?* She noted my discomfort and quickly changed the subject.

"What school do you go to?" she asked, trying to make conversation.

When I told her she replied, "That's where I went to school too. I graduated high school two years ago." We talked some about St. Scholastica's. She did not attend the new campus as it had yet to be built. I began telling her where the new campus was and described to her how it looked.

The new campus was called Cer-Hill, named, oddly enough, after the real estate company that developed it. The school's main building comprised three stories and accommodated more classrooms than the old site, located in central San Fernando, next to the foul-smelling wet market. It was located in the San Agustin neighborhood, an area sandwiched between the center of town and pointed north to the city of Angeles.

The school building had been quite bare when we moved in that early September in 1972. It smelled of fresh concrete, paint, creosote, and various industrial odors from building materials. All the desks and chairs were also new. I remember how much more comfortable these felt compared to the ones we used at the old school, many of which were already there when my mother and her sisters attended in the 1940s and 50s.

Attending the first few weeks was not a pleasant experience. Most of the side roads feeding off from the main highway were unpaved, and dusty during the dry season, but muddy and full of potholes at the onset of the monsoon rains. The dust from these roads and from the empty rice and sugar fields, after the harvest, was whipped up by blustery winds that began in earnest after the monsoon ended sometime in October. The school, being the only building on this side of the street for miles, served as a funnel for the post-monsoon winds, which blustered into our classrooms, blowing doors shut and rattling glass casement windows. If we happened to be walking along the hallways, the winds fluttered our starched and ironed pleated skirts, flapping these up and over our undergarments—we found this somewhat problematic as convent school girls are taught to be modest in all manner of dress. At the time, there was only one male teacher in the school and we naively worried about him seeing us in what we perceived as a red-face moment.

As Annabel and I continued conversing, we found we knew a few Kolasas in common. Then we gossiped about the teachers—our favorites—and the ones we wanted to avoid. This was beginning to feel normal. But was it? The office was large enough for the two of us to settle our cots at some distance from each other. As we chatted, we decided to push the cots closer together in order to hear each other better. It was then that I noticed the color of the room. It bothered me. It was painted a pale green color I had seen in hospitals, and stirred up memories of Timmee, near death at the San Agustin Hospital. Every now and again, a guard knocked and quickly opened the door, checking to see how we were doing. *What's the matter? He didn't seriously think that Annabel and I could squeeze out of those steel-barricaded casement windows, did he?*

The commander's office was not unusually large. There was a massive mahogany desk at one end of the room, and above it hung a portrait of Ferdinand Marcos and another one of a uniformed man I did not recognize. Under the desk was an oriental rug and next to it was a pole flying a Philippine flag. There was a map of the Philippines posted on the wall across from the door. The yellowish light from the ceiling fixtures illuminated the room, casting a depressing glow on the green walls. I avoided looking at Marcos' picture. A well of anger always swelled inside me whenever I saw him on TV or in the newspaper. Knowing he was looking over where I would sleep tonight was like a sword hanging over my head. *Of course they wanted to remind me I could never get away from Marcos' grasp.* When I saw his eyes bearing down on me, he seemed to be saying that he was my guard, my jailer, and my executioner. I vowed not to look at his picture again for as long as I slept in the office.

Annabel, who was speaking next to me with her soothing voice, eased some of the queasiness I felt. *How could she be so brave?* I took note of her features, as if seeing her for the first time, appreciating that she was my only ally for miles around. She had long, dark black, waist-length hair that framed her roundish face and angular jaw. Her dark brown eyes, despite being hidden by equally dark plastic eyeglasses, pierced me—focused and penetrating—as if she could see through everything around her. She was rather short, but she had a physical presence that I found difficult to ignore. Her demeanor seemed fearless. When the soldiers asked her questions, she looked at them with neither cowardice nor apprehension, answering firmly, without losing her calm. Being around her soothed me, if only for a short while.

Then my gaze turned to the windows, where I noticed it had gone dark outside. I looked at my watch. It was after 9 pm. Moments later, she asked, "Do you think we could turn the lights off now so we can sleep?" She said this in a tone like an older sister asking this to a younger one, one whom she senses is afraid.

"Sure," I said, though I felt uncertain. *Did I want that soldier creeping in on us in the dark?*

She stood up, walked up to the switch on the wall next to the door, and turned the light off. The room was instantly cast in darkness but for a sliver of light coming from a street lamp that cascaded gently by the casement window. Lying on the cot, I arranged the bedding tightly around me, hoping to be cocooned against the almost physical terrors gripping every part of my body. Then I started to shiver and shake, drawing the bed sheet and blanket still tighter around me.

My thoughts drifted to home. Ima and Tang were probably getting ready for bed. My sisters, Atching L., Timmee, along with cousin Q., were likely watching TV or maybe doing schoolwork. The twin boys, K. and T. and my older brother, Koyang J., would be on the patio, telling

stories or with friends listening to music. A jolt of pain
shot through my chest as I saw these images in my mind.
My family was only a few short miles away and yet they
might as well have been a million miles from me. It was
as if a cord had been cut suddenly and cruelly. Maybe I
would never see them again. Sleep eluded me that first
night; and did not come easy for many more nights afterwards.

Around six the following morning, I heard a knock on
the door. Before Annabel or I had a chance to say, "Come
in," the massive door opened, a head peaked in and the
soldier from the night before said, "You need to get up. I
have to take those cots away before the commander comes."

We walked the short distance to the conference room
and joined the men for breakfast. The men slept there as
well. The military camp did not have a jail. It was never
meant to be a prison, but it handled the overflow when
Camp Olivas became over-crowded with the hundreds of
political detainees being taken there daily. On my second
day, a young man warned me about Camp Olivas. He had
been arrested once before and was sent there. He said the
conditions there were bad and I was lucky to be here.

"A colegiala like you would definitely have a hard time
over there. You have no idea what it is like to be in Camp
Olivas. You see, when they fed us, there was very little of
it and much of it tasted awful. I was always hungry. The
cells smelled, and so did we. We did not shower regularly
as there were very few showers and with hundreds in the
camp, sometimes water ran out. Sometimes they put five
or six people inside a cell where only two should fit. I
heard screaming nearby all the time, coming from this one
hallway where we were not allowed to go, and there were
a series of rooms, which were always padlocked. Some-

times the screams seemed to turn into howling, almost like the kind of howling dogs do. It seemed to go on forever. Although to tell you the truth, Camp Olivas is not as bad as Camps Crame, Bonifacio, or Bicutan, from what I heard. Being here is somewhat nicer."

How could you expect so little of yourself? What was it really like there? What was it like for you? I was loath to ask him those questions. A part of me did not want to know, a part of me was curious. Then I sensed that he, too, was holding back. He was trying to decide if he should say more. *It must have been really hard.* I kept silent as he hesitated. Maybe he would get the message. I was not ready for more of what he had to say. No more details please. If I showed him that I was not curious for more, he would stop. He did. I was relieved.

While soldiers worked in their offices, we camped in the conference room. When the room was needed for meetings, they ordered us to sit on the floor of the lobby until they were finished. They restricted us to that small space, told not to make any noise and not to talk to anyone who visited the building. Sometimes, they called someone to another room. We knew then that another interrogation was taking place.

Over the course of the day, I discovered that we were allowed minimal reading materials except for weeks old newspapers, a single *Time* magazine, and a couple of Pilipino vernacular magazines called *Tagumpay*. These were passed around so frequently among us that most of them were now in tatters. If we wanted to have a book of our own brought in, we had to give it to the guards for inspection. But few books passed muster and so we read and re-read what we had in the room. Radios were not allowed and so news from the outside never reached us, except the stories whispered by relatives on their visits. I wished I had my school bag. I could at least do my school-work.

There were between fifteen and twenty detainees at any given time in the conference room. Every few days someone from the group disappeared. A fatigue-wearing guard with an automatic weapon (then called an *Armalite*) at his side would come in the room, and soon after whom-ever was sent for would gather his belongings and leave with the guard. Everyone knew he would not be coming back. Was he sent home? Was he taken to another camp? Who knew? No one dared talk about it. Whatever we had known about the prisoner who departed and never returned was left to the world of forgetting. It was better that way. The following morning, a new detainee or two would join the group.

The blur of men's faces was beginning to clear. These men were the regulars who were already here when I arrived and who would still be there when I left. I conversed with them here and there, though I remained cautious. Many were genuine political detainees, I am sure, though I heard that there were spies in the camps. *Probably better not to trust anyone here.*

Two of the men were lawyers. One was taller than the other, and both were of fair complexion. While one talked incessantly, charming us with stories and gossip, the other was quieter, preferring to read. Then there were the two brothers. One was a journalist and the other was a businessman. The journalist was of a slight, lanky build, with short curly hair that frame his bespectacled face. He was never without a cigarette, and was the one who told me to ask my family to bring my meals. He had a confident air about him, and it was probably this that made others suspicious of him. He easily spoke his mind, a defiance that unnerved others in the room. Where the journalist was thin, his brother was portly. He possessed a sunny disposition, and had a penchant for cracking jokes. Both their wives visited daily without fail. It was as though the two wives made a pact to stick together, undertake a ritual, unbroken and unwavering in its repetition. They were the only two wives who visited this much.

Another fellow in the group was a tall and wiry writer who taught at a university. He, too, liked to tell stories. Then there were a few young men in their early 20s. I have forgotten all their names except for Annabel's. But I can still see their faces. In my mind's eye, I can see them squatting on the sea grass mats we called *dase*, which some of them preferred to the metal chairs of the conference table. Many of them chain-smoked. When the odor from cigarette smoke became too much, we asked the guards to open the windows.

Our day was spent in the conference room, punctuated only by visits to the stinky restroom, which was located next to the lobby. Its black and white tiled floor was always wet and muddy. The toilet flush did not work. The pungent smell from it distressed even the commander, whose office was close by, prompting him to order a few buckets to be brought in. Filling these up with water from the lone spigot on the wall, you would need to pour buckets of water straight into the toilet bowl to keep it clean.

Days went by. I was now getting used to the routine. Still, no one told me what I was being charged or if I was charged at all.

One morning, a few of us were, as usual, sitting around the conference table. Others were on the dase, reading the days old newspaper, *The Manila Bulletin*. In another corner of the room, a new detainee was attempting to read the tattered pages of *Tagumpay*. A couple of the men were smoking cigarettes while sitting on the floor and leaning against the walls. They were talking about some movie they had seen, dissecting every part and scene in the film as if they were critics. Their voices got louder as they argued over their favorite scenes.

"Wow, did you see how he was slouched in the bath tub with all his clothes on, looking very drunk, and seeming to be without a care in the world? My, oh my, what acting that was," the writer said.

"Yeah, and I remember how Robert Redford came barging in and saying something clever about this guy being wasted," the journalist remarked.

They were talking about the 1973 movie, *The Sting*, which was very popular in San Fernando at the time. Everyone began speaking at the same time, and becoming louder with each passing minute. Soon a soldier opened the door and told us to pipe down. Everyone became quiet for a while until another topic was introduced. It went on like this, from topic to topic for some time, and then someone mentioned something about the latest thing that Marcos had said.

"Where and when did you get this information?" the lawyer asked.

"Yesterday, when my wife was here visiting. She said she heard Marcos saying on TV that the government had just released the last of the political detainees," the business-man replied.

"Now then, what would you call us?" the tall olive-skinned young man inquired.

There were puzzled looks all around. We were not exactly thieves who stole, murderers who killed, or civil society's miscreants, but since no one has been charged or even told what laws we had violated, we were in a kind of legal limbo. But Marcos did have words to label us. We were *aktibistas*, a term that could either have a positive or negative connotation, depending on whom you were talking with. As conditions in the country worsened, Marcos' rhetoric acquired a nastier tone, and his descriptions of us became more sinister. The names he gave us include, "subversives," "radicals," "Maoists," "Communists," and then to satisfy his verve for political drama, he labeled us the "undesirable elements in his New Society."

We napped when bored, though this was difficult to do in the crowded room. We were prohibited from discussing controversial subjects under the rules set for us by our military captors, so we tended towards small talk. But it was sometimes unavoidable that "hot topic" conversations ensued, like when Marcos denied that there were still political detainees incarcerated. In these instances, we shot each other nervous glances and then more quick looks were directed towards the door to see if anyone outside had been listening. A pall would fall over the room and this momentary lapse reminded everyone where we were and, more important, what was at stake. We wondered how long we would be there, or worse, if we would soon be transferred to Camp Olivas or to the more horrendous Camp Crame in Manila. Quickly, those with enough cheerfulness and confidence would rally the others.

But it wasn't just these controversial topics that kept us on edge. One afternoon, a group of soldiers came trouncing in still wearing their muddied combat uniforms, boots, helmets, and guns. They looked exhausted and ready to sit just wherever they could. Soon another truck pulled up and two men got out. From the back of the truck they took out a stretcher with a body on it. They laid the stretcher down at the entrance of the building so that we could see the bloodied corpse of a man through the window. It sat there for hours. We took turns gawking at the scene before us; I was almost certain what everyone in the room was wondering: *who was this man?* No one seemed to know at first. The soldiers went into the building, not seeming to care that the corpse was going to lie there in plain view of everyone coming and going from the building.

"I am sure they want us to see that," Annabel said. "Yes, probably," I replied with a tentativeness that she now began to expect from me, signaling that I didn't want to talk. My legs were beginning to shake; my hands were sweating. I looked away. I did not have anything more to say, but I knew she was right. They wanted us to see the example he had been made of.

"Let's just go back to where the rest are," I said quickly.

From down the hall, I heard whispers, other people wondering what had happened. I heard the word, 'Olalia' mentioned a few times. Who is Olalia? Was that the man's name?

It was getting close to dinner. Cesar arrived. As with other days, I barely touched what he brought. Tonight, food was the farthest thing from my mind. I thought of giving the food away, as I always did. Back in the conference room, we continued to talk in hushed tones about the most ghastly event to occur since I'd been at the camp. By now, it was common knowledge that a skirmish had taken place in the jungles of Pampanga and Zambales. Or as the military preferred to describe such events, they had an "encounter," as if using a more neutral word would strip away the event's brutality and violence. We heard later that the battle had lasted for hours. The Philippine Constabulary or the 'PCs' as they were commonly called, were intent on capturing the man they had just killed because he, Olalia, was considered to be an important member of the underground.

A few months later, I inadvertently found out more about the corpse of the man I had seen in the camp's front yard that day in December. I found out about it in the place where I least expected to: my mother's kitchen. I was upstairs in my room one afternoon when I decided to go down to the kitchen to get a snack. I found Ima and an older woman, both their heads hung, peeling the skin off boiled tomatoes from a pot sitting atop the tiled counter, and delicately squeezing the skinned tomatoes into pickling jars. Another pot of water was boiling on top of the stove. The woman was explaining to mother when the proper time was for dipping the sealed pickling jars into the boiling water in order to safely preserve them. They were both engrossed in what they were doing, and did not hear me enter the kitchen. When Ima finally looked up, she gave me a smile and said,

"This is my daughter, Vicky."

The woman, her graying hair in a bun and spectacles propped down on the bridge of her nose, looked up and smiled.

"This is Mrs. Olalia, Vicky." The two women nodded knowingly at each other. Mrs. Olalia spoke in a soft voice, sympathetic but not overbearing. She chatted with me about this and that, and the more she talked the more I like her. She was mild-mannered and had an unassuming dignity about her that I appreciated. At some point she looked at me, sizing me up as if she wanted to hug me. *Why do I feel that they are keeping something from me?* Not wishing to dwell on the thought, I concentrated instead on Mrs. Olalia being kind and solicitous of me. They finished what they were doing and sometime later, she left. Over the next several weeks, she and Ima would see each other, mostly at the house, over coffee or tea, while nibbling at some *merienda*[14] that Ima had prepared. They had become fast friends. It was rather strange to me that Mrs. Olalia seemed to have showed up in Ima's life so suddenly. Then after some time, she also disappeared just as quickly.

Then, one day, my mother explained to me who Mrs. Olalia was. She wanted to explain and yet somehow could not do so fully. She was still holding back. But she did say that Mrs. Olalia had two sons who had joined the under-ground and one of them had been shot and killed during a battle with the army. And when she told me the name of the son, it rang a bell. *Oh my gosh! That was the name of the man on the stretcher in the camp.* But I could not tell my mother that I had seen his bloodied corpse. *Spare her the damning details, please.* I did not want her to know what I had witnessed back at the camp. My incarceration was a taboo subject as far as my mother was concerned. She had never asked me how it was for me at the camp; we had not talked about it once. I was not about to start giving her the information that would un-nerve her.

Right then, I realized what it was that these women were keeping from me on that day when I first met Mrs. Olalia. No wonder, knowing looks passed between her and mother. After Ima's explanation, I started to get frightened for her. How could she risk associating with someone from that kind of a background? Did she know she could get arrested

---

14   This word is used in two ways. It means the snack time in the middle of the afternoon. It also means the snacks eaten at that time of the day, usually traditional rice cakes or biscuits with coffee or tea.

too? And where was Mrs. Olalia now? She does not come to the house anymore. *Secrets, secrets. When could we all begin to be honest with one another?*

I wonder to this day how Ima met Mrs. Olalia. Did she seek her out? Did my mother try to find out what it was like with other mothers whose sons and daughters were jailed, or worse, sent to their deaths? Did she look for a way to try to understand what she was going through, only to find that there were countless mothers out there in a similar position? Did it embolden my mother to invite one such woman to come to our house, spend time with her, pickling tomatoes, drinking tea as they shared each other's pain? Knowing now that she did all these things lessens some of the guilt I felt about what I had put her through. The scene of Ima and Mrs. Olalia, working companionably in the kitchen, one teaching the other how to pickle tomatoes, a large pot of boiling water before them, talking in soft voices while drinking tea is a memory I treasure dearly. In my mind, it had become a symbol of hope amid the overwhelming sense of defeat I constantly felt during that period.

I had been at the camp for about a week when one morning, as I settled down on the dase, re-reading yet again the tattered copy of *Tagumpay*, Sgt. Magno came in and told me to follow him. My father was waiting outside. I was glad to see him and even though he looked tired, he greeted me with a smile.

"Listen," he began, "I was able to arrange with the commander for you to come to my office after work so that you could use the shower and toilet there. I understand that there is really no bathroom here." I nodded. "He said that as long as you are accompanied by a guard, you are permitted to walk over to my office. I probably won't be there since the commander prefers that family visits be done here. I instructed the security guard to unlock my office when you arrive. I also told my secretary to leave shampoo, soap, towels, and anything else you might need. I hope you will have a chance to be comfortable, even if only for a bit."

"Thank you, Tang," I told him. "I'm really glad for that. Would it be possible for Annabel to come with me so she can tidy up as well?" I asked.

"I don't know. You will have to ask them, *inang*, "[15] he said affectionately. He then asked me if there was anything more I needed. He was careful not to ask me how I was really doing, I noticed. I didn't want him to ask me anyway. Better to leave things unsaid, I supposed.

After that, in the early evenings, I would walk over to Tatang's office with a soldier escort to use the shower and restroom. Initially, I thought it was because of his position in government that the military accorded me this bit of indulgence, but later I doubted that assessment. I knew that even if Tang had a little more influence than others, things could still go wrong for him.

It was not until I had a conversation with my older sister, C., years later, that I found out why the commander allowed these short trips to Tang's office. Apparently, my father had carefully negotiated with him, convincing him that his office was nearby and that I might as well use it when everyone else had gone for the day. He gave his word to the commander. He also sought the help of his cousin, who was a colonel in the military, and who outranked the

---

15   Kapampangan word of affection to express one's concern to a daughter. It is equivalent to saying, "my dear child." If one were to say the same thing to a son, the word would be '*itu.*'

commander. Rank and status are influential in the military and even more so in Filipino society where things work more fluidly through personal connections. This time was no exception, I gathered.

I remember that visit now. The guard on duty called me to go to the commander's office one morning. Waiting in the room were my father and an unfamiliar man. He was not wearing a military uniform, so I had no inkling about who he was. Father then introduced him as Col. Gomez, adding that he was an uncle. Hearing that he was a relative, I took his hand and kissed it in a traditional sign of respect we gave to elders. I was not surprised that I had not met my uncle before, as I knew from my parents about countless relatives we had never met because they lived in Manila or in other provinces. The two asked me to leave them a few minutes after our brief meeting. I was not privy to whatever they discussed afterwards.

At first, it was a relief that I could now take sufficient care of my personal hygiene when I ventured out in the late afternoon. As the days dragged on, I began feeling uncomfortable and then guilty about this privilege. I felt sorry for the men who stayed behind and ashamed that the commander allowed me this time away from the camp. My escort changed daily depending on who was on duty. Sometimes the guard was pleasant and talked to me while we walked. But, at times, the guard would be silent, refusing to even look at me. Because I never knew what would please or set them off, I became painfully cautious. I developed rules to go by:

Do not talk to them unless you have to.

Only answer what was asked. Never volunteer information.

Be polite but do not let them see how you feel about things.

I practiced these rules because even when these people seemed pleasant enough, I knew I could not trust them.

Every afternoon, when I walked back to the camp following a brief interlude at Tang's office, I would hesitantly enter the conference room where the men were. My cheeks always threatened to redden as I approached them. Then once inside, I kept quiet. I did not want to join in the conversations, preferring to listen patiently in the background, always trying to sense how others felt about me. I would be attentive to what was being discussed and only talked when addressed directly. If they did not address me for a long time, my uncertainty would only grow, reinforcing my worry that they did not trust me. Then it would quickly turn into embarrassment, making me wish I could cover my face like a purdah-covered Muslim woman. They were not long visits, usually lasting about half an hour, but still my guilt persisted. I would turn it over again and again in my mind: *How did the other political detainees really feel about me? Did they hate me? Were they suspicious of me? Did they think I was a spy being afforded a chance to be out even for just a bit when they couldn't?* I had no way of knowing and I was too afraid to ask.

"Stop, stop, don't go there," I would plead with myself while sitting on the dase.

To the men, I was a young girl who attended an exclusive private school, where the rich sent their children. But inside me, I was a piece of rag, one that had outlived its usefulness, torn and ready to be tossed into the garbage bin. I tried to keep my mind blank, tried to stop the thinking so that the terrors afflicting me would relent, even for a bit. I was not always successful. As the dark unknown, so incomprehensible and mysterious, swallowed me, I imagined myself in worn, wet clothes clinging to my shaking body, exposed to the elements, all alone, and shivering in the cold.

My shaking and shivering became unremitting, even merciless, and it reminded me of something that happened long ago. It was Apu Pa's birthday. A big party was underway at the foot of Mount Arayat National Park. The park was a hilly, lush green open space, with a couple of waterfalls and a number of natural pools. It was a bumpy ride from my grandmother's house where we had all congregated to the town of Arayat. The children all sat excitedly, not caring that they were bouncing off each other on the dirt road leading up to the mountain.

It happened like this: A group of cousins and I were swimming at one of the pools when we felt hungry. We began walking towards the grass huts where the adults were laying the tables with food and where a few of the men were roasting a whole pig on a bamboo pole over a pit of red hot charcoals. Along the way, we passed by a small pool filled with green algae, and someone said, "Anyone interested in finding out how deep this pool is?" The boys among us dared the girls, but no one wanted to do it since it was difficult to see how deep the pool really was. Then my cousin, P., said, "I will do it." The boys all cheered. What she forgot was that she did not know how to swim and as soon as she jumped in, she started screaming, waving her hands frantically, and soon the adults heard the ruckus and came to rescue her. When she came out, she was shaking, at once frightened and embarrassed. I will never forget the way she looked. We were all scared for her, but what she had felt must have been worse. It was how I felt when I joined the men in the room after the trip to my father's office. That long-ago image of my shivering, shaking cousin was not much different from me in the conference room.

I wished so desperately for something that would take my mind off the unthinkable. *Close your eyes. Never mind who is in the room. Be still, be still.* Maybe if I keep still, immobile, I can stop this from happening. Maybe this isn't really happening to me.

More than anything, it was fear that consumed me. Being exposed relentlessly to it filled the better part of my day. It competed for my attention, fighting its way in, demanding space inside my poor aching brain. *When will it end?* There, it remained like an unwanted houseguest, refusing to leave. Eventually, I resigned myself to it.

On some days, Annabel was allowed to join me on my trip. I felt relieved on these occasions; walking there wasn't too lonely and plagued by guilt. Those few hundred feet from the camp into the office building seemed like a chance at normalcy for just a bit. It was also an opportunity to rationalize that I was not the only special one on that cool December evening. I could, for a brief time, blur the faces of the men I left behind. Arriving at father's office, we showered and changed. We chatted like old friends, and in the interim it seemed as though we had returned to the ordinary, to the mundane, all of which had fallen out of reach since all this began.

One morning, after breakfast, when we had settled into our daily routine, I noticed that some of the men were whispering to one another.

"Go on," one of the men said to the young man while they gestured in my direction. "Go on, go on, she's not going to bite, you know," he continued.

Several of the men agreed. "Yeah, that's right," they all said.

They kept coaxing him to do something. Finally, he got up the nerve and stood slowly and started walking tentatively toward me. When he was finally standing in front of me, his expression became a mixture of shyness and resolve. He was a rather tall, thin man of about 20 or so years. His dark brown olive skin looked like he was used to being in the sun. He had doleful eyes that seemed like that of a deer finding itself on a road and not knowing what to do. As he handed me a piece of paper, he said, "I made this for you," and his hands started to shake.

"What is it?"

I looked at the paper he had handed me. Unfolding it, I saw it had tiny pink flowers and red little hearts dotting the edges of the stationery. The light pink color of the paper alerted me immediately to its meaning. Back in those days, young men interested in young women wrote them love notes on pink paper to signal their romantic intentions. I felt my face quickly turning red. I looked down at the paper and read what was written at the top of the page. I saw the words, "SOMETIMES WHEN WE TOUCH" beautifully scripted by a hand that relished strong, artistic flourishes and accents. Below the words were the lyrics to a song, that I found out later, was sung by singer Dan Hill. It was a very popular song at the time and a romantic one, far too romantic and mushy for my musical taste as a teenager. Seeing the words on the paper paralyzed me even more. I felt myself go cold, then I trembled, disquieted at the thought that someone was already interested in me in that way. *At a place like this? Now? What was he thinking?*

I did not know what to say. He stood in front of me waiting for me to respond. I tried to look away but the place was too crowded, too small for me to turn my attention to anything other than the male faces staring at me. I looked again at the paper and my hand began to shake.

"Thank you," I muttered, saying it in a voice so weak that even I had difficulty hearing it.

We stood there for some brief and uneasy seconds, both of us uncertain about what to do next. Then he turned and walked back to the group of older men. They started clapping, some high-fiving each other. There were broad smiles and deep laughter in the room of men and one fifteen-year-old girl. I felt myself shrink. I wanted to disappear. *Where was Annabel when I needed her?* The red warm heat of embarrassment continued crawling under my skin and felt hot on my ears. Then my knees began to crumble from under me. I quickly sat down before anyone noticed. I stared at the paper for a long time, not really seeing it, focused on suppressing the tears that I knew would totally undo me. I was not prepared for this. I vowed then that I would not cry in front of these men. *Never. Not in this place. Unthinkable.*

I had felt humiliated at first, and later I became angry. For days afterward, I refused to say a word to him. He greeted me in the morning and I would look at him like he was an inanimate object. Then I would convey to him a blank face mixed with just a bit of frigid disdain. But inside, I was seething.

Young Filipinas in those days were chaperoned when they went out on dates. My fifteen-year-old mind worried that he had broken the rules of propriety. Although I had no reason to believe he wasn't anything but a nice man, as he was generally courteous and even spoke softly, I had become angry out of fear. To have acted out this courtly scene in front of all these men was too much for my very Catholic, conservative convent school upbringing. Even worse, I was afraid my parents would find out. I did not want them to know that boys were already interested in me. My parents did not compromise with us about this. Tang, like most fathers of his generation, believed it was his sacred duty to guard his daughter from the attentive eyes of men, no matter how decent these men turn out to be.

I remember the scenarios only too well when my two older sisters came of age. When young men came courting, formally like tradition required, which meant coming to our house, meeting my parents, introducing themselves, and reciting the long lineage of respectable families they descended from, Tang especially would become unsettled. Sometimes they would even serenade my sisters, which embarrassed them to no end, for by that time, serenading had become an outdated tradition.

At these times, my father would shoo them away, even when my oldest sister was almost 20 years old! But such were the times we lived in. Girls were taught to be modest. Parents guarded their daughters like they were precious, delicate pieces of jewelry, handled with care until they were deemed fit to marry.

In the conference room, thinking about the incident, I felt shivers run down my back and a wild thumping of my heart as if I had committed a crime. I did not want to displease my parents again; nor did I want to cause further trouble. Wasn't I doing that by being here? I couldn't even imagine the grief they were going through. Remembering the combination of disdain, shame, and fear etched on my mother's face while sitting in front of the commander's desk that fateful afternoon, my heart lurched. As for Tang, I was certain he would be disappointed about being unable to protect me as he had done with his older daughters. In my teenaged way of thinking, I figured they were owed the right to be upset when a man began to show interest in their daughter. This was accepted practice with my parents, who had impressed upon us that we should not expect to marry young, for first we needed to finish school, complete a university degree, and then make something of ourselves.

It was only years later did I realize that this was the least of their worries. Like every Filipino household that had fallen victim to martial law, my parents were afraid of the serious and risky position I had found myself in. Would they ever see me again? Would I come out alive? These and a million other things worried them, as Timmee told me later. They were worried that horrific things might happen to me inside, just like they had heard stories of countless women who had been raped and tortured. How silly. Indeed, so silly of me.

I have no idea about what happened to Danhill, my suitor at the camp. I called him Danhill because like the rest of those who were there, I have forgotten his name. Or perhaps my mind refused to give up this secret. Every now and again, when I hear that song on the radio, I think of him. I heard later that he was sent to the larger, more horrific camp. I can only guess what happened to him there. But when I hear this song, I now comprehend at last the stroke of humanity he exhibited at that time in my life. The song will forever remind me of him. That was his song and always will be. He also taught me that life had to go on despite where we were. That life's simple joys, needs, and daily distractions need not stop nor be abandoned just because we were in a place where daily life as we knew it had vanished.

A s the days dragged on, I became anxious to find out when I would be released. The soldiers continued their silence about why I was arrested. What they did tell us was that we are "*aktibistas*" [activists] or sometimes resorted to the more insidious term, "*subersibos*," [subversives]. They were either themselves ignorant about our alleged crimes or perhaps they simply reveled in displaying their power now that the country was under military rule. Translation: no explanation was needed to those whose rights they trampled. And me, a convent-school girl, what did I know about asking them the proper questions about my rights, anyway? I suppose I, too, took it for granted that the Marcos dictatorship arrested bodies: any bodies and nobodies. No one questioned that in those days. We all behaved in ways that people living under a repressive regime behaved—maddeningly uncritical, frightened out of our wits, and mercilessly silenced. And by behaving as such, we unwittingly turned ourselves into accomplices.

The waiting, the senseless, anxious waiting kept me on edge like I was about to fall off a cliff. *What will happen next? The uncertainty of the next second, the next minute. And then what?*

I tried to quiet my mind by reading, but words would jumble on the page, undecipherable and meaningless. My mind was growing fatigued, refusing to function. I looked around the room to see who I could talk to in order to calm my clamoring nerves. I did not find a glimmer of hope on the faces of those around me. Panic only grew when someone was called and he would immediately pack his bag and leave, never to return.

I continued to look for an explanation for my arrest. When I talked about it with Timmee years later, she conjectured that perhaps the military saw me participate at a demonstration, and that the military routinely took pictures of people in anti-government protests in order to arrest them later. She was referring to a demonstration we both attended, which was aimed at protesting recent increases in tuition fees by area schools. "Why then," I asked her, "didn't you get arrested yourself if we were at the same demonstration?"

"I don't know," she admitted.

I have my own speculation about my arrest.

The student activism days that had swept Manila earlier had also reached the provinces. I cannot remember who invited me to attend a sit-in, though I imagine these events had become quite commonplace on school campuses. Curious, I agreed to a meeting at someone's house and joined a group of young people to listen to some lecture on injustice and oppression. The visibly pregnant woman who gave the talk also mentioned some Maoist precepts that as a teenager I found difficult to grasp. At that meeting, she handed out these little red books, the size of novena prayer booklets common to Catholics. It was about a quarter inch thick and was authored by Mao Tse Tung. When I got home and read the book, I found it incomprehensible. I suppose I could have feigned ignorance about being a Maoist because of my inability to unravel its concepts. But that would just have fallen on deaf ears.

As was likely the case with these sit-ins, government intelligence had someone infiltrate this meeting and had reported the names of those present to the military. What I don't understand to this day is that this occurred more than a year earlier, more than likely even before martial law was declared. Why didn't the government arrest me as soon as I came out of the house? Also, it did not answer the question as to what law I had violated in attending such a meeting. We still had freedom of speech at that time as I recall. Surely, one meeting, would not constitute a fifteen year old planning to overthrow a government, no?

How did I violate the laws of the land? How did I become an enemy of the state? I did not ask these questions at the camp because I was certain my jailers would not have told me anyway. Besides, asking them would have been an act equal to suicide, because that would have meant questioning their authority. The situation was dire, that much I knew. How could I not know? By then, the all-too-common images of extrajudicial killings, the military taking extreme liberties with the people they forcibly took, and the repressive power Marcos himself displayed on a daily basis, littered every Filipino's consciousness whether they wanted it to or not.

Repression was increasingly becoming state policy. The military kept getting away with arbitrary arrests and illegal detentions. For many of these arrests, no warrants were ever served. Relatives of those detained were all too frequently ignored when they asked where their missing family members were. They would be kept in the dark for days, weeks, months, or even years. Legally, Marcos had by then scrapped the Arrest, Search, and Seizure Order and replaced it conveniently for him and the military with the Presidential Command Order, a martial law instrument which empowered arresting authorities to arrest anyone without judicially guaranteed processes. The decline of democracy had begun, though there have been many times when I seriously doubted if it had ever really taken root in the Philippines.

Despite the gloom invading my physical and internal spaces, one thing has always been very clear to me. It was the unshakeable resolve that I had done nothing wrong. Knowing this did not assuage the fear creeping into my waking life so that lying on a narrow cot every night, sleep frequently eluded me. I would toss and turn until dawn, when I prepared to face yet another uncertain day. But as terrorizing as the fear that gripped me, there was always that tiny voice inside my head whispering equally tiny bits of hope, making me feel a bit stronger in the knowledge that I had done nothing to be ashamed of. It was this voice that energized me when I most needed it. This energy induced me to continue to dislike, even abhor the things Marcos had done to the Philippines and its people. I could not stand his arrogance, his willful disregard for fairness, and his predilection for violence.

At fifteen years old and lacking the sophistication in understanding the complex entanglements of power and politics in my country, I made Marcos into my enemy. He was an enemy I felt strongly about. Not only that, I made it personal—the only way I knew in order to comprehend what was happening. It was personal similar to the way I would behave abominably with a childhood friend when we had a falling out. How we would profess hatred for one another because we were too stubborn to give in to each other's wishes. I had to put a face to my enemy. That face was Ferdinand Edralin Marcos, the diminutive and cunning man with a booming voice, the president of the Republic of the Philippines, once called the Strong Man of Asia, the dictator who imposed martial law on the country and who sent thousands upon thousands of Filipinos to prison or to their deaths because they were opposed to the way he was running, or rather, ruining the country.

This time, as sleep eluded me again, I began to feel hatred. It was palpable hatred that I could have sworn I could feel running physically through every bone in my body. Perhaps it could have made me ill had I let it. The shaking and shivering I frequently experienced I now realized was a mixture of both fear and anger. But this hatred was no longer the juvenile anger, the temporary kind that I displayed towards a playmate. It was more akin to rage. This time, I saw Marcos as the face of the evil that was running amuck in the place I've called home. I even knew to think that the men who sent me behind bars were of minor importance. They were simply doing Marcos' bidding. Marcos, the more I thought about him, was the single manifestation of the villainous road the country had taken.

We could not speak our minds for fear of being labeled as spies. The journalist who had spoken freely was perceived as one of these spies when he encouraged others to do the same. He was charming enough and I did like him. But if I had been friendlier and less cautious, I would have violated the rules I made when I was arrested. It was a shame that I had to keep my distance, but the longer I stayed there the more I saw the need not to trust anyone. Sure, I felt a certain kinship to those in the conference room. I even liked them, though it was important that I did not show it.

When did I begin to think like this? What was becoming of me?

Martial Law Philippine Style

The image that millions of Filipinos saw on television was a grainy, fuzzy portrait of an austere-looking Ferdinand Marcos. Wearing his familiar *Barong Tagalog*,[16] Marcos faced the camera from behind a desk. Only the top half of his body was visible. It was unusual to see him sitting. We were accustomed to seeing him behind a lectern or standing by his massive wooden desk with the presidential seal above him.

Something is wrong with this picture.

Marcos' image was lopsidedly framed on the screen, as if he was sitting close to the edge of the chair. The room was dimly lit and it was difficult to tell where he was. The darkened room contributed to the aura of toughness Marcos projected through his facial expression.

Were they intent on scaring us?

Tension was thick as my family gathered in front of the television. We knew an important announcement was going to be made. It had been announced earlier that Marcos was going to appear on national television.

---

16   The Barong Tagalog is the traditional formal attire for men, usually made of a flimsy or sheer fabric either of cotton blend or the more expensive *piña*, so called because it is woven from pineapple fibers. The outfit is usually intricately embroidered in the front.

Why was the presidential seal missing? Was Marcos even at Malacañang Palace? Did they not want us to know where he was? I reasoned that perhaps it was hurriedly put together. Then Marcos spoke:

> *As of the 21st of this month [September 1972], I signed Proclamation No. 1081 taking the entire Philippines under martial law for one purpose alone, to save the republic and reform our society.*

Then the screen went blank interspersed only with white noise. Martial law: the two dreaded words that instantly became Marcos' shield against his own people loomed upon us. It was these words that put his enemies in jail. It was these words that silenced the whole nation. The swiftness with which the adults saw the implications of this pronouncement was displayed immediately in the worried looks on my parents' faces.

Hoping to see if we could find out more, my brother, N., switched to another channel. There was nothing. He tried another. Again, only the incessant white noise was heard, only the same black and white lines waved forlornly across the screen.

"Let's turn on the radio," Tang suggested.

"Yeah, let's put it on *Radyo Patrol*," I said. This was the radio station we listened to for updates during the floods we had experienced just two months earlier.

"I have it on now. I'm searching but I'm not getting any reception," N. said.

We quickly congregated by where the radio was. My brother rotated the radio dial, and the box started emitting static. He continued turning the knob through the AM band and then again through FM. The radio frequencies simply buzzed.

I saw my father's worried expression as we sat around on our rattan sofas and armchairs in the living room. He furrowed his brows as he looked down at nothing in particular on the floor. This was his usual expression when he was thinking hard. There seemed to be a lot on his mind. My mother was quiet, but she, too, could hardly contain her anxiety. Hands clasped tightly on her lap, her eyes looked sadder, more fearful than usual.

My mother was prone to thinking the worst. I had seen her usual worried face over the years. By the time my siblings and I were old enough, we had all become accustomed to her nervous behavior. She always seemed tense, her breathing almost asthmatic, and was easily panicked. On many nights, when dusk settled, darkness has fallen, and Tang had not come home from work or a trip, her fear only grew. She would pace back and forth, and would then march nervously toward the sliding Capiz-shelled encrusted Yakal-wood windows of our house, scanning the street for signs of father. I learned to do this from her. She must have taught me well because I became nervous or anxious with increasing regularity, as I grew older.

To be fair, I recognized that my mother had experienced the violence and cruelty of the Japanese when they occupied the Philippines during the Second World War. An aunt once told me a story of Ima, a teenager during the war, and her participation in rescuing Filipino and American soldiers during the Bataan Death March, sometimes hiding them under their floor-length skirts called *sayas*, unceremoniously discarding their sense of modesty in order to save a hungry, fatigued, or dying Filipino or American soldier. I can only imagine how terrifying that might have been for anybody, but particularly for a young, convent-school-bred woman, because had any Japanese caught them, they would have suffered the grim consequences of rape, followed by torture and then death. It would not be misplaced to suppose that she now thought martial law meant Filipinos would suffer a similar fate as they had lived through under the Japanese.

My thoughts began to wander again, puzzled as to why Marcos waited two days after signing the declaration to announce it to the country. I never figured this out. Years after enduring that period of my life, I became too memory-scarred to revisit this question. When I left the Philippines, it was one of those things I consigned to the dust and rubble of history because to attempt to answer it would have meant stirring up the pain and reopening old wounds.

Meanwhile, as I sat with my own thoughts, I turned my attention toward my parents who, at that point, were looking at each other with unease. They were probably wondering how much to tell us. Perhaps, they never really knew where to begin, particularly among their younger children. By then, my three older siblings had departed for Manila either for work or for tertiary schooling at the university. The younger ones stayed behind with the oldest being in high school. Finally, Tatang, a man of few words, spoke.

"As far as I know, although I am not an expert on this," he began, selecting his words carefully, "when the military takes over private communication networks such as radio, television, the newspapers, etc., then it is not business as usual. Our country will be going in a very different direction from now on, and most likely, things will be very different from what we have known. We will just have to pray to God that it will not be as bad as it appears now."

Tatang was right. For days after the pronouncement, no radio or television station broadcast. The once privately held radio and television networks were the first businesses to be seized. The Lopez family-owned ABS-CBN was the most visible execution of Marcos' media takeover. I found out years later just how it transpired. An interview with Eugenio Lopez, Jr., the son to the former owner of the same name, for a documentary film on martial law, recounted how it happened. On the day that the document transferring ABS-CBN to the government was signed, the older man refused to even read it, Mr. Lopez, Jr., related. In his words, the conversation between his father and Marcos was brief. It went like this:

"Mr. Lopez, it seems you have not even bothered reading the document," Marcos said.

"If I disagreed with any of these conditions, would you revise it?" replied the senior Mr. Lopez.

"I don't think so," acknowledged Marcos.

"Then, what's the point?" Mr. Lopez allegedly retorted. He then took the paper and signed the document, effectively giving up the largest broadcasting network in the Philippines at the time to government control. Shortly thereafter, the network was turned over to Marcos' crony, Roberto Benedicto.

And so began Marcos' control of newspapers, radio, and TV stations as part of his military rule. Aside from ABS-CBN, Benedicto was also given a newspaper and radio stations to manage. A newspaper, whose name I can't recall, was effectively banned in my family. We could not imagine reading it. As we complained back then, "Why would anyone read something published by a Marcos' puppet?" Every time Benedicto's name came up in family conversations, we never failed to pair it with the word, "*tuta*," whose original meaning in Pilipino is 'puppy dog' but which in slang meant a lap dog, a crony, or someone who is blindly obedient.

We found that the usual program offerings had been expunged, as stations slowly were brought back on air. In their place were bland and boring reports coming straight out of Malacañang, the presidential residence. The popular news anchors on Philippine television were replaced by the all-too-frequently seen image of Francisco "Kit" Tatad, the presidential press secretary. Every time he went on air, it was to announce the newly signed letters of instructions, executive orders, and special decrees from the president. I still retain a distinct memory of this short, unsmiling, bespectacled man with thick lips and dark black straight hair, martial law's most visible representative and its most loyal agent.

"*Oya na naman ing digpa ning alting tuta ng Marcos*," (There goes that Marcos yes-man again. May he be struck with misfortune), we would bitterly complain and then promptly switch the TV off. At best, Tatad was Marcos' official spokesperson. At worst, he was the one solid, or sordid, if you will, representation of a system gone mad.

Marcos subsequently signed more than 3,000 of these decrees and executive orders during the course of his regime. There were so many that it was puzzling to me how Filipinos could keep track, or even be aware of them. They would surely not remember them if, like my family, they turned off the set when Tatad routinely took over the airwaves.

The largest newspaper at the time, the Roces family-owned *The Manila Times*, was also taken over. From then on, the editions published were unrecognizable in terms of the spirit and style of the newspaper we had enjoyed reading in the past. Other newspapers like *The Manila Chronicle* were also controlled. A new national paper also appeared although it was never regarded as genuine journalism in my family. We all agreed it was more of a Marcos propaganda tool. All along, Marcos' plan was to restructure Philippine society because, as he claimed, the country needed saving. Strong words. What we could not have known was that the new society that he installed was more repressive, cruel, and violent than the one he discarded.

As Tatang talked, it dawned on me that if Ima's thoughts had been about impending cruelty and violence, she would not have been wrong. Daily life took on a grim and menacing quality, especially during the early years of martial law. No, my mother was not wrong at all in thinking the worst this time. She did not live to see it end. Although her passing in 1976, less than two years after I was released from political detention, was one of the most painful events we endured as a family, it was perhaps fortunate that she did not live to see the misery and the downward spiral the country has taken under Marcos' regime.

Media companies were the first to go but this was only the beginning. Other industrial enterprises were also seized and handed out as rewards to those who loyally supported him. Having granted Benedicto a big slice of the media pie, he began giving away other companies, first to immediate family members and then to his cronies. The names Cojuangco, Floirendo, Tan, Disini, Romualdez, and Cuenca were bandied about so often in gossip as well as in official news sources, that their names, to my mind, were synonymous with martial law Philippines. When one talks banana monopoly and banana plantations, the name, Antonio Floirendo, was uttered in the same breath. When infrastructure development and the Construction Development Corporation of the Philippines, or CDCP, as everyone called it, were mentioned, the name Rodolfo Cuenca came up. As for automobiles, Ricardo Silverio was the man who revved up its corporate engines. Herminio Disini was tied to tobacco and cigarettes. But many say the biggest and closest crony to Marcos during this period was Eduardo Cojuangco, Jr., who dipped his hands in coconut plantations and also claimed as his own, the Ayala-owned and the country's largest, San Miguel Corporation. Cojuangco, in a move to consolidate and secure his power, eventually controlled two monopolies: MERALCO for electric power, and PLDT for telecommunications. Years later, after Marcos died, his wife Imelda and their children would try to take over these companies, instigating a protracted legal fight which has not been satisfactorily resolved to this day.

It is worthwhile noting here that Cojuangco is a cousin of Corazon Cojuangco Aquino, the woman responsible for finally toppling Marcos in the first People Power revolution in 1986, three years after the tragic assassination of her husband and Marcos' nemesis, Benigno Aquino, Jr. This is the way politics was played in the Philippines then and one can venture to say it is the way it is played even now as Cory's and Benigno's son, also named Benigno, took the reins of the presidency in 2010. The Philippines has been routinely governed by a few prominent Filipino families who are, more often than not, interested in political power as a means to secure and maintain their economic interests.

Later, the name Lucio Tan became closely associated with the nation's dominant carrier, the Philippine Airlines. He was Marcos' friend and partner in crime. The daily newspapers splashed pictures of the two and other crony friends playing golf at the Wack Wack Country and Golf Club or places where the rich and famous gathered. Crony capitalism has begun in earnest. In my teenage mind, these men were the accursed enemies.

Marcos' predilection for corruption and, subsequently, for violence, had started long before he placed the country under martial law. I learned early as a young girl that this was a man who had been accused of murdering his father's political opponent. Tried and convicted, he was later pardoned by former president and WWII Japanese collaborator, Jose Laurel. I remember this story because the adults in my family talked about it when Diosdado Macapagal, a fellow Kapampangan, lost to Marcos in a presidential election in the mid-1960s. By the time of the 1969 election, Marcos had strong-armed his way to reelection using goons, guns, and lots of money. He outspent his opponent in the dirtiest election the country had seen, keeping in mind that Philippine elections were generally dirty, dishonest, and violent. An article published in *Time Magazine* expressed precisely this sentiment upon reporting on the events of the 1971 Plaza Miranda bombing. It began,

> *Settling scores with bullets rather than ballots is nothing new in the Philippines, where personal vendettas are frequently settled in the heat of campaigning.* [17]

It could not have been put any better. In this regard, Marcos was no exception; in fact he hijacked elections and became a master at it. By the end of his second term, he was keen to remain president despite the prohibition of third

---

[17]   *"Binding up the Wounds,"* Time Magazine, November 22, 1971.

terms in office as stipulated by the constitution. He set up a constitutional convention to amend the constitution that would then pave the way for him to stay in power. He also orchestrated events in order to convince Filipinos that the country was balancing on the brink of political and economic collapse. He further escalated his play for power by resorting to even more violent tactics in hiring goons to bomb public places. He sent in the riot police into rallies and demonstrations even if these were peaceful and legal. It was said that he hired people to intentionally create chaos in these public protests so he would have reason to arrest its organizers.

One of the defining events of this period was the Plaza Miranda bombing, the same event reported by the *Time Magazine* article. I remember it to this day as one of the most horrifying events of the period before martial law. On the evening of August 21, 1971, the Liberal Party, the opposition counterpart to Marcos' Nacionalista Party, staged a *miting de avance*, a final political rally before the elections. Congressional and local elections had already been scheduled to commence just a few days later. As the speeches began, two grenades were tossed onto the stage and seriously injured prominent Liberal Party members like Senators Jovito Salonga and Sergio Osmeña, Jr., as well as Manila mayor, Ramon Bagatsing. I listened to the news on the radio and waited anxiously for the program host to announce who had died. My family was loyal to the Liberal Party and strongly supported its candidates for this election. The bombing killed nine instantly and injured about a hundred in the audience as one of the grenades had landed where the crowds were gathered. Senator Benigno "Ninoy" Aquino, Jr. was one of the key speakers of the evening, but had narrowly escaped injury because he had yet to arrive when the grenades exploded. Speculations abounded that Aquino was a principal target since he had become a pain in Marcos' backside.

Around this time, the underground dissident movement also began to gain traction. The January 30, 1970 student demonstration, known as The First Quarter Storm, resulted in the deaths of four students. The First Quarter Storm— so named by student leaders and activists of the period, and which emerged out of the tree-lined avenues and hallowed halls of the state university and exclusive private academic institutions—signaled the unfolding social and political strife. Many upper- and middle-class students comprised its leadership and ranks. After the bombing, its membership increased dramatically, as did its dissident activities. The armed counterpart of the Communist Party known as the New People's Army or NPA took advantage of the country's instability. At the time, I thought they were not capable of the same violence that Marcos exacted on his enemies, and I admit that I was sympathetic to their cause. I was not alone. Countless Filipinos sympathized with them even if they were afraid to say so. People were tired of Marcos' political manipulations and were hoping that the underground movement presented a just and humane alternative. Evidence began to surface in the post-Marcos years that the left was not exactly innocent of violence and brutality. Some have even speculated that they were responsible for the Plaza Miranda bombing, though the accuracy of such an accusation remains a long-standing and divisive controversy. Increasingly, the two sides blamed each other for every bombing and riot, which were growing more frequent in many parts of the country. While the NPA waged war against the government in the countryside, Marcos began orchestrating a war against a growing number of Filipinos whom he saw as disloyal.

With the line on both sides of the political spectrum clearly demarcated, civilians were caught in the crossfire. For many, this untenable situation only made it easier to take one side or the other. For others, they were left without a choice, easily becoming victims of atrocities committed by both sides. Soon, we saw a country sliding away from the kind of democracy envisioned by Americans when they handed Filipinos their independence after the Second World War.

Many Filipinos believed that the Plaza Miranda bombing was a watershed moment in the country's political history—violence, savagery, and brutality had intensified to a previously unseen level. It remains a mystery to me as to who was responsible but in the following year, Marcos declared martial law. In the ensuing months, Marcos did not simply make a policy of repression; he institutionalized it. By 1973, when soldiers picked me up at my school, I too had become its victim.

Prior to declaring martial law, Marcos suspended the writ of Habeas Corpus. I remember my family sitting around the dinner table one evening, with the adults having a vigorous discussion about the meaning of the writ of Habeas Corpus. As I listened, I wondered what these words even meant. These sounded like big words to me and so I decided to look them up in a dictionary. *How were they even spelled?* I needed to ask a grown-up. Flipping through the pages of an old dictionary, I looked for the phrase, "writ of Habeas Corpus." 'Writ,' according to the dictionary, was a "legal document, which prohibits." I guessed it must be something related to legality, but what it prohibits, I could not guess. Then I looked up the phrase, "habeas corpus," and discovered that it meant that "a prisoner be brought before a court at a stated time and place to determine the legality of detention or imprisonment."

So suspending the writ meant what again? I asked myself again and again. I was annoyed at my inability to understand. I was fourteen years old at the time and I hoped that I would understand it better when I was older. I did not have to wait too long. Soon, some of the most prominent politicians of the opposition, student leaders, labor activists, farmers, priests, nuns, etc., found themselves in prison, as the writ faded from my mind.

Not long after the writ's suspension, massive flooding inundated Central Luzon, a region that included my province, Pampanga. It is difficult for me to forget these floods even now. The loss of life, the destruction of property, and the devastation of a wide swath of natural resources caused great suffering to hundreds of thousands of residents. An extended monsoon period brought lengthy and massive amounts of rain.

Older folks in our neighborhood complained bitterly about our denuded forests, which they claimed contributed to the flooding. They believed just as their ancestors did, that trees helped in preventing floods. Others criticized the ineptitude and corruption of politicians and government overseers, but more importantly, decried their inability to build and manage efficient waterways and sewage systems that could divert the floodwaters. Though some water canals had been built, these were used to dump garbage because trash collection was never done on a regular basis. Thinking about it so many years later, I am transported back.

I hear the sound of water splashing, whirling, and battering Apu Pa's house. It's been raining for days now. Rains like we've never seen before. Monsoon rains, from around May to September, are usual at this time of year. Farmers favor the monsoon; it signals to them that the rice- and sugar-growing season has commenced. Throughout the low lying plains of Central Luzon, which is the country's major producer of rice, sugar, and other grains, it is common to see farmers, bent over in rice fields, planting seedlings in muddy paddies with their legs steeped in sludgy water that rose midway up their calves.

This time it is different. These are not the steady rains that last for days and cease when the tropical sun comes out again the next day. The rains come in wild torrents for hours at a time. And then there are only brief let-ups in-between. Then the rains fall again, battering everything in sight. It seems as though the rains are angry, carrying on an indefinite temper tantrum. Weeks go by. The grounds are saturated. Water has nowhere to go. Then the floods came.

The sound of rain hitting the metal roof of Apu Pa's house turns into a constant background noise. The raindrops are big, forming fog-like as far as the eye can see. I decide to venture out of doors. I am desperate to be out for I am tired of being kept indoors. I can hardly see in front of me. My umbrella is useless. The rains are now accompanied by strong winds. My umbrella buckles from the rain's pressure, its ribs splitting away from the water-resistant fabric. The umbrella hangs limply in my hand. I am soaked to my skin and can't wait to get back inside.

Big, heavy raindrops keep pounding the region. Flood-waters continued to rise and so did our apprehensions. Water seeps into everything. I now see houses tumble.

People in them have nowhere to go. Many have already taken shelter in schoolhouses and other public buildings. Government officials say they can no longer accommodate any more people. We keep our ears tuned to news reports from Radyo Patrol, the program that has become our lifeline for information. There is no good news. Imang Dandy's favorite program host, Orly Mercado, reports seemingly non-stop, traveling across the region but telling the same story again and again. Flooding, rains, and more rains expected. The crisis intensifies and so does Radyo Patrol's reporting.

Both Apu Pa and Imang Dandy are now worried that the floods will soon reach our neighborhood. Sure enough, water begins flowing into the first floor of Grandma's house, a sturdy, well-built house that has stood on the same spot since the turn of the last century. Water begins to seep in first through the crawl space below the ground floor despite the sandbags piled at the gate. Imang Dandy, with her wet *kimona*[18] clinging to her body, stands in a foot of water in the kitchen. She directs my cousin, R., and me to start removing furniture and appliances. We scramble to get it done, barely managing in the nick of time. Luckily, the second floor of the house is spacious enough to bring up the extra furniture and furnishings from below. We asked male neighbors to help us in lifting the bigger appliances. All of us are now soaked and exhausted.

The floodwaters, which were only about an inch high hours ago, have now reached a depth of about five feet inside the house. I stand at the top of the stairs on the second floor. The only thing I can see is the upper part

---

18   A *kimona* is a woman's traditional blouse, which is usually embroidered and worn together with a loose printed cotton skirt for informal daily wear worn around the house.

of the walls and the ceiling of the floor below. The water itself is muddy brown, not unlike the river water we see at the back of the house. I can see that the Pampanga River has overflowed, sending its waters into all the houses along its banks.

I change into dry clothes and tune once again to Radyo Patrol for the latest. It is not much better in other places, the radio reports. Flooding has now consumed the plains of Central Luzon. From the province of Bulacan on the southern side of Pampanga, the waters are skirting north and northwest towards the provinces of Nueva Ecija, Bataan, and Zambales, leaving no place safe for miles and miles.

The young sugar and rice seedlings planted just a month ago are now under water. Farmers will not be able to harvest these at the end of the season. Old trees are uprooted. Small nipa-style houses made of bamboo and native grass—the preferred dwellings for peasants—are collapsing on top of their waterlogged foundations. News of families abandoning houses and seeking shelter in public schools reaches a frenzied pace as local authorities discourage people from these overcrowded places. Schools are ordered closed indefinitely. No one knows when classes will resume.

In early September of 1972, we headed back to school after almost two months of continuous rain and flooding. The new campus at Cer-hill was hurriedly completed because the old site was still under water. We were barely at the new school for three weeks when Marcos declared martial law on September 21. School was closed once again.

On the morning of the first day that classes resumed, I remember that it was unlike our usual school routine. We were standing in line on the quadrangle singing the national anthem as two students were raising the Philippine flag. After the usual announcements were made and instead of marching to our classrooms, Ms. Arceo, took a PA system in her hand and announced,

"You are not to go to your classrooms at this time. We will let you know when it will be appropriate to enter your classrooms. Stay in the quad until I tell you to go. Do not break out of queue and stay within your own class. I do not want to hear talking at this time."

Everyone wondered what was going on. We looked at each other, asking questions in whispers. It was puzzling to us why we weren't allowed back to our classrooms. We spoke in soft voices when the teachers weren't looking because we knew better than to displease Ms. Arceo. We waited patiently in line in the quad as the sun began to peek through the somewhat cloudy sky. Our teachers walked away and headed into the building. Minutes later, they appeared, each holding a big yellow-brown envelope, the kind that had a red cord tied to its flap.

"All teachers need to be with their assigned homeroom classes at this time. Inspection can now begin," Ms. Arceo announced.

Teachers filed past the student lines asking each student to open their school bags. They inspected each bag and every metal object such as scissors, nail cutters, tweezers, and anything that had a blade, no matter how dull it was, was taken and then placed inside the envelopes. We were then told that these would be kept under lock and key. We would only be able to use them with permission from teachers and only during approved activities such as Home

Arts and Home Economics classes. *Was this how martial law was going to be from now on? They would not even allow us to use dull scissors to cut paper in class?*

This is weird, I remember thinking. The world that we knew had changed. We were uncertain and somewhat apprehensive about what lay ahead. School was different now. *What else would be?*

In the first days, weeks, and months of martial law, thousands were sent to prison, shuffled from one military camp to another, slammed in detention centers, and tortured in safe houses. Many of these arrests were arbitrary, without proper arrest warrants, with detainees incarcerated for long periods of time without being charged. Some of those picked up disappeared without a trace. They died either by being shot or succumbed to the injuries they sustained from torture. All were thrown in unmarked graves. In some cases, tortured and mutilated bodies, the handiwork of Marcos' torture units, were mercilessly dumped on roadsides for public display. Students, priests, nuns, artists, businessmen and women, laborers, union organizers, factory workers, farmers, fishermen, and just about anybody who they suspected was anti-Marcos, were seized in homes, schools, businesses, churches, rice paddies, farms, markets, or anywhere Marcos' foot soldiers searched for their prey. No place was safe. Hundreds more will be put away over the succeeding years.

The Spanish word, '*desaparecidos*' did not appear in the Pilipino lexicon, but this phenomenon happened just as it did in Latin America. Instead of desaparecidos, "salvaging" was the word used to describe acts of kidnapping or picking up a detainee, taking them into "safe houses" for torture, making them suffer through harrowing investigations, and finally ending with the victims being mutilated, decapitated, or shot. As in Chile and Argentina in the 1970s, many bodies were never found.

Contemplating on the word, "salvaging," I am distressed by the incongruity with which the Philippine military reversed its original definition and corrupted it with a callous and contemptuous connotation to describe what they do to "enemies of the state." Moreover, the phrase, "safe house" was another aberration of lingo, which in martial law took on its opposite meaning. Safe houses were clandestine places, usually motel rooms, private residences, or cells in military barracks, run by intelligence operatives, that were in reality torture chambers. These safe houses struck fear in every citizen because we all knew what transpired in these places. Salvaging cases increased through the martial law years, a phenomenon seen by human rights experts as contributing to the breakdown of the rule of law and the rise of military terrorism in the Philippines.

'Solitary confinement' was another phrase I heard frequently. Senators Ninoy Aquino and Jose Diokno, the military man turned rebel, Victor Corpus, and captured NPA leaders, Bernabe Buscayno, alias Commander Dante, and Jose Maria Sison, were the most prominent figures who suffered through this particular form of coercion.

Charges of subversion, indefinite detention, the increasing use of military tribunals, and the growing cases of military lawyers prosecuting civilian cases in civil courts (leaving political detainees with very little legal maneuvering) were all too common occurrences. Cruel and inhuman punishment was made official policy under

Marcos with activists sometimes suffering a fate worse than that reserved for criminals convicted of heinous crimes.

On top of this, Marcos once brazenly announced, "No one but no one has been tortured," while Amnesty International was simultaneously interviewing dozens of detainees and preparing reports to be sent to human rights organizations around the world. Then, compounding this deceit, he claimed that there were no more political prisoners, a statement he announced in light of an upcoming Papal visit. This demoralized the families of those waiting to hear from their detained sons and daughters. Amidst this repressive display of abuse grew a pernicious culture of denial in which, to this day, very few if any, soldier, general, or Marcos crony has been prosecuted or punished.

By the account of Alfred McCoy, a professor of history at the University of Wisconsin, military murder under the Marcos regime was at the "apex of a pyramid of terror, with 3,257 killed, 35,000 tortured, and 70,000 incarcerated."[19]

Seeing these statistics, I realized I was a mere number among many.

Years ago, I read the following passage in a book:

...the violence enveloping the country erupted on all fronts, completing a development that had began in 1964 with the appearance of the first guerillas, trained in Cuba by one of Che Guevarra's aides-de-camp. Coexisting in Argentina were: rural and urban Trotskyite guerillas; right-wing Peronist death squads; armed terrorist groups of the large labor unions,

19   Quoted from a talk given by Prof. McCoy titled, *"Dark Legacy: Human Rights Under the Marcos Regime,"* given at a conference, Legacies of the Marcos Dictatorship on 20 September 1999 at the Ateneo de Manila University. This talk was also extracted from his book, *Closer than Brothers: Manhood at the Philippine Military Academy.* New Haven: Yale University Press, 2000. This exact quote was taken from a reprint of the talk produced online and can be found at http://www.hartford-hwp.com/archives/54a/062.html.

used for handling union matters; paramilitary army groups, dedicated to avenging the murder of their men; para-police groups of both the Left and the Right vying for supremacy within the organization of federal and provincial police forces....[20]

This passage is from Jacobo Timerman's account as a political prisoner during the rule of the military generals in Argentina in the 1970s. Timerman, a journalist, newspaper publisher, and person well known to the Argentinian elite, was arrested by the military junta in 1977, four years after my own arrest. Reading the above passage from his book, *Prisoner Without a Name, Cell Without a Number*, I thought that if someone were to read the passage to me without invoking Argentina, I would have said without a doubt that the author was talking about the Philippines during the time of Marcos. It is not surprising to me that the political affairs in Latin America mirrored those that occurred in the Philippines during the same period. But what I find incredulous is this: truth and reconciliation commissions in these countries were established aimed at uncovering the truth, with the purpose of identifying those buried in mass graves, thereby providing some comfort to victims' families.

No such truth commission, excluding the one set up to recover what the Marcoses have stolen from the Filipino people, was ever put in place in the case of the Philippines, despite the fact that Marcos has since left the country and died. No person who participated in atrocities during the martial law years has ever been punished. What is it, I asked, that makes Filipinos different from Latin Americans

---

20   Timerman, Jacobo. *Prisoner Without a Name, Cell Without a Number* (New York: Vintage Books edition, 1988), page 13.

in confronting truth? Why do Filipinos not find the need to rectify what was done to its citizens and to the country? Do they not care? What has happened to their sense of civic responsibility, not to mention their moral and ethical obligations? Has their fear obliterated their spirit? Why, I wonder, can't they be more like those in other countries who have sought the truth and justice for those who have suffered?

There is, I observe, an uncanny similarity between the savagery of the military juntas in these Latin American countries and that, which was perpetuated by the military under Marcos. It is understood that some of these South American soldiers were trained in the United States. The same can be said of some Filipino generals trained by Americans. It was these generals and military elites who sharply demarcated the lines between them and us. 'Us' are the "*madlang tao,*" (the hoi polloi) and them—the soldiers who spilled the blood, the cronies who ran away with the country's riches, and appropriated it as their own, and those in government service who abandoned their civic duty and responsibility as caretakers of the people.

Decades later, as Latinos, and consequently, the Rwandans, and South Africans willingly confronted the dark periods in their history; the Philippines glaringly ignored its moral obligation to seek the truth. This is the country that showed the world in 1986 that they could overthrow a dictator peacefully and without bloodshed. It was a shining moment for the country.

Now, it needs to embrace a shining moment once again.

It would be so once the country could bravely look at its past in order to salvage what could be saved in a culture of violence and willful disregard for humanity.

I read Timerman's book long after I left the Philippines. It was not possible to read it while I was still living there, as it is not a book that was available under martial law. Besides, my subconscious would likely not cope well with a book that contain images so disturbingly and hauntingly similar to the ones I saw, heard, and experienced in the Philippines in the 1970s. As I read books like Timerman's, I began to see myself in the stories, and harrowing as the experience was, it paved the way for me to begin unearthing the feelings and experiences I buried long ago. Alicia Partnoy's book, *The Little School*,[21] in her tales of disappearance and survival illustrated that stories similar to those in the Philippines were not rare. As I read her short tales, they triggered flashbacks of what I had seen and heard: a man with a bloodied shirt and fresh gunshot wounds was found in the rice fields one morning as a farmer awoke early to tend to his crops; a young man in denims and a T-shirt with his rubber flip flaps missing from his bloodied toeless feet, his corpse callously dropped and splayed across the highway. Vehicles had to swerve to avoid hitting him and his body became gored beyond recognition. Then there was a body whose head was covered with a black cloth tied with a string around its neck. It was discovered in the shallow waters of the Pampanga River, the same river running behind my parents' house. A classmate, who left for school one early morning, saw a spectacular burst of fire from a car parked in front of the school. There was a man burning inside. By the time I arrived at school that morning, all that remained was a raging fire that had once

---

21   Partnoy, Alicia. *The Little School: Tales of Disappearance and Survival.* (San Francisco: Midnight Editions/Cleis Press, 1986).

been a car and a man. Then there was Olalia's corpse at the detention camp's entrance.

As for desaparecidos, I knew someone who disappeared too. I was barely a teenager when it happened. My aunt, whose part-time business was running a small fleet of jeepneys as public transportation vehicles, plying the towns of San Fernando and Mexico, was upset one day because one of her drivers failed to show up for work and was still missing after several days. She heard through the grapevine that he had been abducted. His body was never found.

A few years ago, while doing research for this book, I returned to the Philippines, and while there, I visited an organization called the Task Force Detainees of the Philippines. It is a non-profit organization that advocates for the rights of political prisoners as well as it provides their families with support and other types of assistance during their incarceration. In addition, TFDP regularly reports on the status of political detainees, and the extent of extrajudicial killings that continued to occur even after Marcos had been driven from power. One particular book that caught my eye as I was visiting their library was entitled, *Pumipiglas*.[22] Turning its pages, I read accounts of torture experienced by those who were picked up by the military over the years. It also described the conditions under which detainees lived out their incarceration. Some detainees in a Davao del Norte jail, for example, endured

---

22   Pumipiglas in Pilipino means struggling to be free. Like a bird that is struggling to be free from someone's grasp, it is also used metaphorically to describe political struggles. It is also the title of a report published by the Task Force Detainees of the Philippines (TFDP). See *Pumipiglas: Political Detention and Military Atrocities in the Philippines, 1981-1982.* (Quezon City: TFDP, 1986).

... the practice of dumping political prisoners in small cells together with prisoners charged with murder, homicide, theft, robbery, drug-pushing and the like. There were no health facilities to speak of. The sick were simply referred to the jail administration, which only looked into emergency cases. Water had to be coaxed out of a rundown water pump.[23]

While I was able to have my meals delivered by my family during my incarceration, many were not so lucky. Detainees in Lanao del Norte experienced the following:

No breakfast.... For prisoners there is really no such thing as a regular 11:30 lunch. The guard in charge arrives at his convenience. One cup is given to each prisoner to cook for himself. Once a week, they are served a little meat. Nothing else is given; no salt, no vegetables .... On top of these, very often, the prisoners do not get fuel to cook their food... They have to eat the rice half-cooked to save fuel for the next cooking.[24]

Recalling the conversation I had with my cohort at the army camp and his description of the life led by detainees in other military camps across the country, conditions like these seemed implausible at the time. But as I spent more time at the library, I realized he had been telling me the truth. As I went through pages and pages of these accounts, I came across countless instances of military abuse. Reading through the accounts, I discovered similarities: the methods used to extract information from the victims, the brute force of their interrogations; all one

---

23   Pumipiglas, page 43.

24   Pumipiglas, page 43.

can do is ask: why? Change the names and the places; the story is the same.

Among the most notorious agencies of the military was the Philippine Constabulary, or PC for short. To me, it simply cannot be mentioned in the same breath without invoking martial law. The members of the Philippine Constabulary were not soldiers who protected Filipinos; they were Marcos killers, on the front-line positions of Marcos' war against his own people. They were his assassins who sought out revenge and exacted retribution against members of the underground, or those simply suspected of harboring dissidents. They were the murderers who bragged about their brutal slayings, with Marcos promptly awarding them with military medals of honor or courage, which after a time catapulted them to the top echelons of the military. The zealousness with which they discharged Marcos' orders contributed a great deal to the country's descent into savagery. Partnering with para-military units, the most infamous of which was the CHDF, or the Civilian Home Defense Forces, they became martial law's lethal "weapons" in dispensing pain, suffering, and brutal death to the opposition, or to anyone they deemed unsympathetic. It was once again ironic that the Marcos government gave the name Civilian Home Defense Forces to this para-military group. CHDF was no friend to civilians. I heard many personal accounts of disappearances in Pampanga and other places, all perpetuated by the CHDF. Later, Marcos went even further by integrating the national police into the military. From that point on, state sponsored terrorism eclipsed the rule of law.

The realities of the political instability of the 1970s were well known, especially to those who suffered in its hands. Whoever takes the care to peer closely at the time and space where chaos reigned, soon learns that alternatives for accord were running out. The solution, in many cases, was to seek out options elsewhere, preferably outside of the country's borders. By the time I graduated from university, I knew it was time to leave.

Faces of the Enemy

D espite the well-fortified and deeply financed Marcos arsenal of repression, insurgency was inevitable. Marcos could not have been a more effective poster boy for recruiting young people from cities, towns, or barrios into the underground movement. Each and every atrocity committed by the government inflamed more of the country's disaffected youth, provoking them to join the ranks of those who fled to the hills. The remainder of the Philippine population endured instability, uncertainty, and frustration. On top of all these, poverty prevailed.

If the Philippines were a theatrical stage, in one very small corner would stand the growing ranks of the disaffected, crowded together but muzzled, and given little voice. In another, slightly bigger corner, were the weakened and browbeaten workers in government service, who were expected to nod and cower, as Marcos remained imperious. Members of the military and Marcos' cronies occupied a third and much bigger corner. Finally, occupying the largest corner was Marcos himself and his wife, Imelda. From a theater enthusiast's vantage point, there was only one conclusion to be drawn in the unfolding political drama: the destructive path of authoritarianism had begun. Conjugal dictatorship,[25] was, as a former Marcos ally called it, the name of the game. No agreeable option to provide even just a sliver of hope brightened the horizon. The omnipresent image of Marcos wherever we turned became invasive. We could not criticize him publicly, yet within the privacy of our homes, we cursed him when we saw him on TV or heard him on the radio. My aunt, Imang Dandy, a fiery, tomboyish woman who never married, was an influence on me regarding political matters when I was young. She was intensely passionate about politicians she liked or hated. If she liked a politician, she became his or her biggest fan and cheerleader. If she hated one, the politician might just as well be the devil incarnate. Marcos belonged to the 'hate camp;' her reason being that not only was he corrupt but he had cheated in the election against Diosdado Macapagal. Her loyalty to a fellow Kapampangan outweighed any attempt at a fair regard for the facts. In this, she was no different from the average Filipino voter whose allegiance to ethnic identity trumped the appeal of democracy. She was an avid radio listener but when she heard Marcos' voice come on, she would grouse in her no-holds-bar manner of speaking, "*Itak naiada na ning alang marine a yan. Aitu ne naman qng radyo. Macabuysit yang darandaman. Patdan mu ne pa at e me sisidian cabang magsalita ya ing animal a yan!*" (May misfortune strike that shameless scoundrel. He's on TV again and it is annoying to hear him speak. Turn the thing off and don't turn it on again for as long as he is speaking.)

---

25   Conjugal dictatorship was the term used and the title of a book written by former Marcos ally, Primitivo Mijares. He later defected and rumored to have been assassinated by Marcos' henchmen.

Perhaps because we did not know any better, or perhaps it was our belief in her that us—her nieces and nephews—and willing converts, would quickly distrust politicians that she did not like and adore those she did. At a germinal level, we were beginning to learn our lessons in politics. But more than this overly simplistic tutelage, what she, and countless others were unleashing, I later realized, was their frustration and discontent, given the destructive, corrupt, and almost nihilistic version of government practiced by those in power.

There were innumerable images of Marcos gracing the newspapers and television during this period. He was often seen wearing his crisp and formal Barong Tagalog. Perhaps because he was not a tall man, and therefore would not do justice to the "*Americano*," as Filipinos referred to the western men's business suits, he rarely wore one. But what he lacked in physical stature, he more than compensated for it in an over-abundance of confidence. Possessed of a stentorian voice, he was adept at modulating his tone and inflection at the appropriate moment, making people perk up and listen to him. Whether Marcos was aware of this or not, politics, for him, made great theatre, and he was a commanding actor on stage. He occupied the spotlight on the stage of Philippine political theater for more years than was comfortable for anyone. The political arena seemed custom-tailored for him given his penchant for manipulation. He was just as comfortable with crowds of poor farmers, reassuring them that their side was his side, while later he would dance the night away with the privileged class, many of whom were invited regularly at Malacañang. He might have been convincing had he invited these farmers to those fabled luxurious soirees and extravagant parties hosted by Imelda. But, of course, he never did. Mixing the two groups was not politically advantageous; keeping them separate would ensure his grip on political power, pitting each group against the other when it was convenient for him to do so.

Though Marcos' voice was firm and deliberate, it was his eyes that gave him away. He had Asiatic, crafty eyes that often, or deliberately, one might speculate, missed their target. In my recollection of those images of him on TV, he never looked straight at anyone. His were shifty eyes that conveyed his proclivity for falsehood.

Marcos was also rumored to be a womanizer. It has been said that if politics is around the corner, libido is never far behind. The combination of sexual and political power has been the domain of politicians and public figures throughout history. Marcos as a politician was no exception. I remember well how I disliked the way he smiled, the crinkle on his lips, a gesture between a smile and a sneer. The smile was lecherous, a smile that replaced many an indecorous word when directed to the opposite sex. For that reason, his marital infidelities regularly greased the rumor mill. How could any Filipino of my generation, or the one before me, forget his affair with the American starlet, Dovie Beams? Her picture graced the gossip pages of periodicals at the height of their affair. We reveled at hearing this gossip and stories like it because there was not much we could say freely regarding fact in a repressive public arena. Inane as it may sound, there was much private humor we could derive in the image of a strong man with a penchant for dropping his pants. How about the Filipino actress who allegedly had acid thrown in her face by Imelda upon learning of her husband's marital indiscretion? Unfortunately, his many affairs and conquests of women only served to incite traditionally chauvinistic Filipino men to beat their chests and boast their male virility, never apologizing for it because they believe it was their God-given right to behave that way.

Aside from this, Marcos was a smart, shrewd and sly politician. He combined this with, as my husband loves to say of men who are so full of themselves, "an ego the size of Texas." Before Ronald Reagan was dubbed 'the great communicator' when he became president of the United States, there was Ferdinand Marcos, who, by the late 1960s and into the 1970s and 1980s was adept not only at manipulating, but in controlling the media. He understood that communication networks were critical in his ability to tighten the noose around a people in an archipelagic territory composed of thousands of islands whose natives spoke a wide variety of languages and dialects. Twisting facts and then presented as truth was the rule rather than the exception across radio and television stations, newspapers, and magazines.

Marcos was often conveyed via the media wearing his signature Barong Tagalog and making pronouncements about the new society. That was as much civil society one got in those days. He dispensed with the legislative assembly and muzzled the courts, thereby eradicating any branch of the government designed to balance his power. Silencing any opposition from other branches of the government meant his ability to trample the rights of citizens was unfettered. Goons, guns, and gold—all were at his disposal in a despotic reign that lasted close to a generation.

Internal political opposition as well as Western scholars and writers later confirmed my youthful view of Marcos' character. For one, Stanley Karnow, a journalist who spent many years working in Asia and knew some of the Philippine elite, described Marcos as a "grand master of manipulation." In his Pulitzer Prize-winning book, *In Our Image: America's Empire in the Philippines*, he contends that as early as a year before Marcos declared martial law, the then US Ambassador to the Philippines, Henry Byroade, had known that Marcos was "jockeying to cling to power after his term expired in 1973."[26] Despite Marcos blaming the Communists for bombings, Karnow claims that some of these were actually his doing. One of these bombings destroyed the sewage system of suburban Quezon City. The author wrote that the CIA had been reliably informed that Marcos' henchmen were responsible. He explained that Marcos enlisted the help of the "Rolex Twelve," a dozen men who had been given this moniker because Marcos rewarded them with Rolex watches when his plans of mayhem were successfully executed. His aides and executioners were, over the course of his term, endowed with a zeal for persecution that sometimes put their Holy Inquisition counterparts to shame. As I got older though, I reflected whether the reason for this was because these men truly believed in what they were doing or rather that they dreaded Marcos' retaliation had they refused.

Among the plots staged by the Rolex Twelve was the assassination attempt on the then secretary of defense, Juan Ponce Enrile, the same man who defected and supported Corazon Aquino in the 1986 People Power Revolution, and who would, years later, admit that the assassination attempt was a scam. I remember this story

---

26   Karnow, Stanley. *In Our Image: America's Empire in the Philippines*. (New York: Random House, 1989), page 356.

particularly well because at the time, Enrile's daughter, Christina, was at the secondary school of the college I attended before I transferred to the Jesuit-owned Ateneo de Manila University. At that time the nuns at the college circulated a memo to all the students to pray for Christina's father. This incident and other similar stories were fodder for late-night whispers and gossip. We found it difficult to talk about them much except with immediate family. When we did, it was through jokes we invented based on these events, using humor as a release from the stifling atmosphere of politics.

Marcos best played the game by playing it dangerously. He fabricated a Communist threat, which to this day, has not materialized, to stifle opposition in all its forms. He attacked his enemies with every intention of exerting deep psychological intimidation and long-standing degradation. In addition, he justified his use of unprecedented presidential powers, taking advantage of the severe flooding that devastated Central Luzon and claiming that the severe economic consequences of the floods required extraordinary presidential expediency. Experts on Philippine politics also believed that Marcos was emboldened enough to execute his brand of coercion and repression because he had the backing of the United States. If I remember correctly, it was not until Marcos' final days in 1986 that Ronald Reagan sent a team with Senator Richard Lugar and diplomat Philip Habib to tell Marcos that it was time to go.

For years, never a day would pass without us seeing Marcos' picture in the newspapers, hearing his voice on the radio, or seeing his image on TV as he went about his day at the presidential palace, Malacañang, with the best video clips reserved for the nightly TV news. His images and those of his wife, Imelda, dominated on-air television. There was hardly any speech or meeting given by Marcos that was not broadcast. Switching to another channel was an exercise in futility given that all of the stations showed the same thing.

There were unforgettable TV moments, for sure, those that one dared not watch because they were either too shocking to be true but were true nonetheless, or those that simply made one sick because of their untruths and fabrications. Or yet again, those that made it look as though Marcos was winning the war against his enemies—those faceless Communists, leftist rebels, subversives, and radicals he kept talking about but whom we rarely saw except as bloodied corpses on the same nightly news.

One of these stories was the capture and arrest in 1977 of one of the principal founders of the Communist Party of the Philippines, Jose Maria Sison, or "JoMa" as he was known. This was reality TV, Philippine style. Marcos milked the event for all its worth. There was Marcos, seeming to stand tall despite his diminutive stature, affecting gestures to show everyone he was boss, speaking to dozens of reporters with military men swarming all around him, recounting how the communist leader was captured. It was an image not easily forgotten. No one I know, or for that matter, few of my fellow countrymen included, knew what the most wanted man in the Philippines looked like before his capture. It would be fair to say that some even doubted whether he was a real person of if he was simply a figment of Marcos' imagination. His capture confirmed that there was such a man. This event might have been the beginning of the end for the underground movement, though history would prove this not to be the case.

As I watched the spectacle of this broadcast, I did not know whether to feel sad or disappointed. The face of JoMa Sison, the one every freedom loving "aktibista" in the Philippines revered, could not have been more disappointing. Watching him on TV, I wanted him to look big. I wanted him to look masculine. I wanted him to look as menacing as possible because I needed such an image to counter the overwhelming image of Marcos the tyrant. I needed to see a Rambo-like figure that would stand in contrast to the defeat and disappointment we experienced daily, someone that would lessen the sense of defeat and humiliation I felt when I was taken prisoner. But Sison was the complete antithesis of Rambo. There he stood, flashed across the TV screen: a wiry, lanky, and bespectacled figure. He was more like an intellectual than the shaggy bearded Che Guevarra-like fellow in combat fatigues with an AK-47 at his side. I carried this disappointment with me for a long, long time.

This disappointment rivaled my dismay a year earlier, when I watched the capture of Bernabe Buscayno, the alleged chief Supremo of the New People's Army in August 1976, which took place in a town called Mexico, just a few short miles from my parent's house. Popularly known as Kumander Dante, he was born and raised in Tarlac, a province to the north of Pampanga where the natives also spoke Kapampangan. Tarlac had once been part of Pampanga and therefore it was not surprising that the two provinces shared common agrarian and linguistic traditions. He grew up in a peasant family, with a father who had abandoned them when he was young. I remember the whispers and hearsay in San Fernando when he was captured. Mexico was only a ten- to fifteen-minute drive from where I lived. It was a topic of conversation among

Kapampangans when he was captured and detained in Camp Olivas before he was sent to Camp Crame in Manila. I remember my surprise in learning that one of the government's most wanted rebel had been sleeping a few short miles from us. I did not even know that he was Kapampangan. Television, newspapers and radio had a field day with his capture. To some degree and despite his capture, I felt pride in him being a Kapampangan.

Marcos' utilization of the media continued for as long as he was in power. But not to be upstaged by his constant media presence, his wife, Imelda, became an even bigger example of media's power and influence. For every media feature of Marcos, there was one of Imelda. There was Imelda in her brightly colored *terno*,[27] often being ushered through a crowd of well-wishers, with a bouquet of flowers in her arms as she reached out to shake hands. She smiled, she waved, she shook hands—all gestures of a celebrity, a role she performed with such drama and aplomb. She, in her heavily made-up face, her perfectly coiffed hair, and brightly colored ternos, did justice to the Filipino formal attire, using it as a necessary appurtenance in her charm toolkit, so like the beauty queen she had been. The Marcos crony-controlled media also made it look as if people could not get enough of Imelda.

There she was again, Madame Iron Butterfly, as she was by then called by the Western media, this time, in a yellow sequined and embroidered affair, shown leading a group of luminaries to some garish building she had just built. She had a certain fascination for constructing all

---

27   The *terno* is the traditional formal wear for women, best known for its very stiff butterfly shaped sleeves. It is a gown historically made of a fine, flimsy and delicate material called *jusi*. The *jusi*, when cut into a terno, is almost always embroidered with fanciful designs of leaves, flowers or traditional symbols.

kinds of buildings. One of the first was the Philippine International Convention Center, or PICC, a structure built on reclaimed land on the banks of Manila Bay. Then there were the Heart Center, the Lung Center, and then the Kidney Center, displaying a strange fondness for internal organs. More Filipinos, however, were familiar with the Cultural Center of the Philippines. In an interview for a documentary, Imelda, sparkling in her diamonds, wearing a formal blue and yellow affair and a coiffed hairdo, sat on an expensive-looking sofa and a gilt-edged console filled with family photos and a bust of Ferdinand Marcos behind her, spoke these words in Tagalog about the CCP.

> *Iyong Cultural Center, iyon ang parang.... [This Cultural Center, this is like] our monument to the Filipino soul and spirit. Doon natin ilalagay and lahat ng kagandahan ng ating [this is where we put all of the beauty of our...], the good, the beautiful, the right of whatever we have through the course of centuries....[28]*

I remember the fanfare that ensued when she inaugurated the CPP. She invited many international celebrities and public figures to the event. Her propensity to live big and spend big became unquenchable. It was parties galore in the streets of Manila for the rich and famous. But there was a dark side to this type of glamour, Imelda-style. She hated for her privileged friends to see the city's poverty, so she erected fences around squatter areas, preventing her and the city's privileged caste, the bold and the beautiful, from seeing the disagreeable sights and smells of poverty-stricken Tondo or other slum settlements. Beauty and ugliness always shared equal space on Manila's streets, but Imelda

---

28   This quote is taken from the documentary film, *Imelda*, by Ramona Diaz and aired on PBS in May 2005.

insisted on only acknowledging the former. Her mania for surface beauty seemed to grow in proportion to her phobia of destitution, hardship, and deprivation, pushing her into creating an artificial and contrived world in which the Philippines was a paradise of beautiful women (and at times for sale) and physical structures built from a growing national debt. She spoke about this again in the interview for the same documentary and said,

> *I remember when he became president. I asked him. Ferdinand, now that you are president, what is my role as First Lady? He said you are the First Lady and the mother of the country, while I Ferdinand is the father who builds the house. You make it a home and so I had to reflect what makes a home. Love. Now what is love made real? Beauty....*[29]

For all the beauty that she relentlessly tried to showcase by building structures that will signify economic progress in a poor country, she had simply been reduced to one thing today and it is what the world knows about Imelda: her shoes.

It had become common knowledge in those days that the Marcoses used the country's treasury as if it was their own personal bank account. Years ago, I heard a story about Marcos' extravagant spending from a fellow passenger on a plane. I was leaving the Philippines and sitting next to a well-traveled American man who once worked for the United States Information Agency. As we introduced ourselves and started talking, he recounted to me a story about Marcos. He began by saying that he had a friend who had established his name and reputation in

---

29   Quote also taken from the documentary film, *Imelda*.

public relations. This man became quite popular among politicians and purportedly advised President Nixon on communication strategies during Watergate. Ferdinand Marcos had apparently heard about him and hired him to help improve Marcos' PR image in the Philippines and abroad. The man did his job and Marcos was reported to be very satisfied with his work. Shortly before boarding his plane, and upon his departure from the Philippines, four men carrying machine guns, all strangers to him, approached the PR man.

"Sir, you forgot your briefcase. Here it is," one of the strangers said and tried to hand him a briefcase.

"No, I didn't," the PR man answered. "I have it right here," he continued and proceeded to show them his briefcase.

"No, sir, this is your briefcase," insisted the stranger carrying the other briefcase. "Sir, this is your briefcase. Take it," he said more firmly.

The PR man reluctantly took it, and minutes later, boarded his plane. After he found his seat, he became curious about its contents. He opened it gingerly, not knowing quite what to expect. It was then that he saw stacks of cash, filling the briefcase to the brim. He had already been paid for the work that he did, but this was his reward for doing exactly what Marcos wanted.

We heard many stories of Imelda's extravagant shopping sprees, where she spent millions of dollars in a single day on her visits overseas. We joked about it between friends, as the two plundered the country. But in truth, their trickery and dishonesty was no different from people smelling the odor of rotting fish in the market. Like rotting fish, their profligacy stank, and the stench was impossible to conceal. Everybody knew about the deception, though we did not know what to do about it. We dared not even talk about it in public, particularly in the early days of martial law. But the stink was never far away.

Many said that the Marcoses had a marriage of convenience. Whether or not it was true, the "conjugal dictatorship," they forced on Filipinos kept the couple in power for years. To my teenage mind, Marcos claimed full ownership of the dictates of tyranny and despotism. Never mind that such despots like Papa Doc in Haiti, Idi Amin in Uganda, Moammar Gaddafi in Libya, and the military juntas of Chile and Argentina were forcing similar regimes to their own peoples in other parts of the world. Those other despots did not influence my young life. It was the despot Marcos who did.

As for Imelda, her vanity and hunger for material things were insatiable. She lived in splendor while the poor masses were left living under bridges and scavenging the Smoky Mountain garbage dump for food and scrap to sell. The budding feminist in me cringed each time she waxed romantic about the famed Filipino woman and her beauty. I later on realized that she used beauty to mask her delusions about both the country and her own humble origins. Surface beauty, in her mind, could cover up the rot that was engulfing the Philippines.

I am reminded of an anti-smoking poster ad I saw in a women's washroom years ago. The message read, "Smoking stinks no matter how you dress it up." Next to this was a picture of a beautiful woman, perfectly made up and looking very classy, but with a cigarette stuck to her mouth. The takeaway: No amount of sprucing up could make up for a rotten core. Smoking is never a good idea; but so was Imelda's attempt to beautify everything thereby rendering contempt for the ugly, the sordid, the macabre, the despicable, and the unspeakable. In many ways, she was not unlike many Filipino women, who are reticent in talking about difficult subjects, even when the consequence of not doing so was their own suffering, physical or otherwise. Many of these women preferred to suffer their indignities in silence, leaving it to God, or so they prayed, to be their sole judge and avenger. Their silence helped create an environment ripe for injustice or exploitation. Imelda maintained, even in her older years, and long after Marcos was overthrown, that her husband's imposition of martial law was something good.

There was no Filipino executed under martial law even if he was convicted of murder or given a death sentence. Walang Pilipino (No Filipino). That was what martial law can be proud of. It was a compassionate society and it was a benevolent leadership...[30]

She went on to say,

We never had such a terrible violation of human rights. In fact, we had no human rights case whatsoever here in the Philippines.[31]

For someone with this moral turpitude, Imelda was apt to say anything of a husband who would keep her in the lap of luxury, and in a position of immense power. She showed little regard for the thousands that were killed and the more than 70,000 incarcerated. One could make a case that both Ferdinand and Imelda suffered from psychological complexes, and that the excessive powers they bestowed on

---

30   Quote is taken from a documentary film produced by the Foundation for World-wide People Power called *Batas Militar: Martial Law in the Philippines* that can be viewed in 11 parts on www.youtube.com.

31   As quoted in PBS documentary, *Imelda*.

themselves made abuse and corruption inevitable. As for me, the effect of my own lingering wound, at that point, had gone much further than I could ever imagined. It also became the mask that I preferred to wear instead of facing the truth about what truly happened to me as a political prisoner under martial law in the Philippines.

I believe to this day that Marcos needed to be brought to his knees in the same way he brought the country to its knees with violence and savagery. It must be said that the Philippines was no stranger to cruelty, as they endured the beastliness of colonial rule by three different countries over a span of more than three hundred years. But even such a long-suffering and overly patient people have their limit. The 1986 People Power Revolution saw to that. After more than twenty years, Filipinos were ready to replace Marcos.

I never met Ferdinand or Imelda personally, yet they invaded the physical and mental spaces of my life for such a long time. It is time I would not have given them voluntarily. By making me one of the thousands of political prisoners, they became the center of hate, of the turmoil that resided within me after I was sent to prison. I found it difficult to see myself as a victim because I had always seen myself as a plucky girl. But it would be foolhardy not to acknowledge that I was indeed a victim. Indeed, I acted like one and hated myself for it.

Yet, despite the pangs of victimization I felt, it was harder still, when I heard so many stories of people, and more specifically of people I knew, who suffered terribly at the hands of the regime. Political prisoners during that period, it is now acknowledged by human rights experts, tended to suffer worse than those handed down prison sentences upon a conviction of a serious crime. With this knowledge, I hated Marcos all the more. The more I saw their images on TV, the more I felt the anger personally. Perhaps I did not know any better. I was young, shaken, and psychologically wounded after my incarceration. Could one really hate so much, I asked myself as I got older. Why did I think that they were evil personified? It was not until I was much older and long after I had left the country that I did what I should have done all along: pity them. Of course this revelation came only after so many years of being unable to let go of the anger and the hate.

Years after I was released, I remained afraid for both myself and for the countless others who suffered similar fates. In my own reckoning, the prison I faced was not only the one with the four walls in the camp, but rather in my own mind. I was convinced that true freedom was no longer a possibility. How could I not think this when we were not allowed to speak our minds? How could I not believe this when there were times I felt that my movements were being monitored? As repression escalated, so too did my angst. So too did the national angst. The country's collective psyche was damaged and it would take a long time to repair it. I long ago accepted that it was not a healthy one to begin with. Even before Marcos, Filipinos had long suffered at the hands of colonial masters: the Spaniards for more than 300 years, the Americans for more than 50 years, and three years of brutal Japanese occupation during WWII. By the time all three entities had left this archipelago country, we'd lost any sense of national pride and of truly owning our destiny. When Marcos unleashed his repressive tactics on a people who had already been subjugated, vanquished, and tyrannized by former colonial rulers, the result was a population that was brought to its knees.

It is also a country whose adults often failed their children. I came to this conclusion because of what happened to me when I was fifteen. When I look back and ask myself why Ms. Arceo at my school allowed the soldiers to take me away, I am saddened by the knowledge that here I was failed. When I reflect on why the Marcos government could not distinguish between a true radical and a girl of fifteen, who could not have plotted subversion nor would have the means to overthrow a government, I realize that adults failed in their role as protector. When the adults around me preferred only to remember the young girl who was arrested, then again the adults failed. I had become, as Toni Morrison once wrote in the foreword to her novel, one of those children described in *The Bluest Eye*.

The death of self-esteem can occur quickly, easily in children, before their ego has "legs," so to speak. Couple the vulnerability of youth with indifferent parents, dismissive adults, and a world, which, in its language, laws, and images, re-enforces despair, and the journey to destruction is sealed.[32]

The faculty at St. Scholastica's Academy failed to protect me as a student who innocently thought she was just going to school that day and never imagined that it was going to be the backdrop behind which her world would turn upside down. Other adults in my community chose not to wrap their arms around me, when after being released

---

32   Author Toni Morrison, in the foreword to her novel, *The Bluest Eye*, said that when she began writing the story, what she was interested in was not in the resistance to the contempt of others, but rather to the "far more tragic and disabling consequences of accepting rejection as legitimate." Her characterization of this type of rejection by adults is the thing that I have found to be the most paralyzing particularly in children, who are just learning to come out of their own and to experience the world in their own terms, but then this journey is cut short due to no fault of their own making. As for me, while the destruction has not been as complete as Ms. Morrison suggests, it has certainly felt that way at times.

by the military, I was desperate for warmth, both physical and emotional. Their silence in my presence and their hesitation to be around someone who had been labeled an enemy of the state were far removed from the cultural mores and practices Filipinos are so proud of with regards to protecting one's own blood and preserving the spirit of family and community.

As I reflected on this experience years later, I realized that there exists a form of duplicity in the Filipino value of strong family bonds and reality. I would even argue that this duplicity has much to do with the Catholic religion and the way in which it permeated our entire language and culture. This realization dawned on me one day when I was conversing with my sister, Timmee, about certain aspects of the Filipino culture. I mentioned the extreme prudishness of many Filipinos and how this attitude, for example, has seeped through the language.

"What is the word," I asked my sister, "for a lady who becomes pregnant without being married?"

"*Mesira yang dalaga,*[33] " she said.

"Yes, that is correct," I replied. "Isn't it interesting how we describe her in that way? To invoke the word, 'mesira,' which as you and I know means 'broken,' aren't we allocating a non-value to her? She no longer has value because she lost her virginity and with it her prospects for being married. Being mesira to me has a kind of finality about it. That is the concept, as we know it in Kapampangan. 'Mesira' cannot be fixed. But we all knew, when we were growing up in the 60s and 70s, that calling

---

33   This was how a woman who loses her virginity before marriage and gets pregnant was described. It literally means broken woman. *Dalaga* is the Kapampangan word for a young woman, a maiden.

someone, "mesira yang dalaga," also implied that nothing more could be done about it. She is broken and cannot be fixed. She cannot be touched and she will go on to raise her illegitimate child, who, like herself, will be ostracized and made a pariah. It was a judgment we imposed on them because, in our minds, they broke not only the rules of propriety; they also were not good Catholics. And the priests of our church never admonished us for treating women like this. How sad."

The image of the shunned woman in town, like Hester Prynne in *The Scarlet Letter*, was what I had become after prison. Though I had not gotten pregnant, I somehow began to understand how these women felt, for I, too, was 'mesira,' i.e., broken, unfixable, and suffering from no small amount of low self-esteem.

But I also knew this: the adults who preferred to see me only as the 'one who was sent to prison' not only failed me as a child but also made them accomplices to the cruel and savage world created by Marcos. As I got older and my political knowledge deepened, it became clear to me that the violent actions of the government imposed a debilitating effect on the administration of justice. This crystallized my belief that a government, which wages a war on its own people rather than protecting them, is a government created out of malice and greed. Adults have failed. The government has failed. Caught in the middle were people who were far too often rendered helpless and, consequently, became lost souls. It was even more disheartening for me to think of the possibility that every Filipino in that dark period abdicated any sense of responsibility towards our shared human condition.

As an adult, I comprehend that there will be times when we will fail our children. We will err in their rearing as our parents erred in theirs. But the mistakes we make, I always hope, would be the kind that would not smash the spirits and the true nature of our children. I take the view that these mistakes can be turned into learning opportunities for both parents and children.

The most tragic of the consequences of my incarceration as a young girl and the one that proved to be the most difficult to regain was the loss of my free spirit. Along with me, there are thousands of Filipinos who suffered the same fate and whose journeys to regaining their true nature are not yet complete. To my mind, the legacy of martial law and the repressive Marcos years will always loom large and will overshadow whatever attempts are made to seek the truth and to carry out justice. I also believe that it will be a continuing disservice to all Filipinos if there is no serious attempt to confront the truth and punish those culpable from that inglorious period in history. We are all still waiting, though four presidents have taken office after Marcos was thrown out of power. Moreover, some of the extrajudicial killings during Marcos' time continue to occur in some parts of the country to this day.

The Other

Early one evening, just a few days before Christmas in 1968, my family was about to sit down to dinner, when an aunt, my mother's younger sister, barged in unexpectedly and slumped down on a kitchen chair. She was pale and looked visibly frightened. Following behind her was Cesar. Usually a calm and quiet fellow, he too looked agitated.

"Could someone please give me a glass of water," pleaded my aunt. Someone quickly got up from the table and granted her request. Earlier that day, my aunt, a grocer in town, had asked to borrow the vehicle along with Cesar to take care of some business.

"We were driving on one of the streets in Villa Victoria when a truck pulled up and stopped in front of us," she began. "They blocked our way and Cesar was forced to stop. Four men quickly got out of the vehicle. I could not see their faces as they were covered with black cloth with just slits for their eyes. They pointed their guns at us and demanded that we hand over the Jeep. They said they would not harm us if we give it up without a fight. I was shaking so much I could barely get out of the Jeep. Cesar came around to my side to help me. They took the keys

from him and just a few minutes later, they were gone."
She paused then continued. "We were at the edge of Villa
Victoria, next to the rice fields and it was very dark. I am
sure the men chose this spot because there were no street
lights around," she lamented.

"I have never been in that place before and I was scared
too," Cesar added.

"How did you get back to town?" someone asked.

"Cesar and I walked a few blocks until we saw lights on
the main highway and waited on the side of the road until
we were able to catch a *calesa*.[34] Thank God, we did not
have to wait for long till one came along," she replied.

They related more details about what happened, but
told everyone that it would be very difficult to identify the
thieves and that only one spoke.

"Did he speak in Kapampangan or in Tagalog," another
relative asked.

"It was in Tagalog," my aunt said. "I was so nervous that I
couldn't tell you if he was native Tagalog or a Kapampangan
speaking in Tagalog. Or he might have been Ilocano. Who
knows? Maybe Cesar would have known if the guy spoke
with a Visayan accent."

"I don't know. I was too scared to notice," Cesar said.

We sat around the table, quietly transfixed by their story.
Soon, as we recovered from the initial shock, assurances
were uttered, everyone comforting my aunt and our driver
that they were now safe and out of a dangerous situation.

Christmas won't be a lot of fun this year, I thought,
what with Ima losing the vehicle she needs for her business.
We all felt gloomy as dinner was served. My aunt cried as

---

34   A *calesa* is a horse drawn carriage still used as public transportation today in San
Fernando.

she told my mother how badly she felt about losing the Jeep. Despite reporting the theft to the police, it was never recovered. We found out later that similar car thefts had occurred in recent weeks. We also heard that while there were known vehicle thieves operating in that area, members of the underground movement were involved too. The rebels were allegedly selling the vehicles to finance their operations. We never found out who was to blame, but time and again, we heard other stories like this: either in the form of vehicles being stolen, or rebels forcibly taking over land and farming it to feed their growing army. I do not possess adequate proof that the left condoned these crimes, but these stories persisted when I was growing up.

To this day, one hears similar stories, despite the town having evolved into a prosperous city. In 1968, my mother's vehicle was stolen at gunpoint. In more recent years, my family was subjected to criminal wrongdoing at the hand of leftist rebels. This time, a group of armed rebels laid claim to a piece of land in the village of Kulubasa in Pampanga that has been in my family for generations. Tang had loaned it to his brother to farm, until one day, these men visited him and demanded that he surrender the land to them. My uncle had no choice; they apparently told him that it would be best that he cooperate or else. That "or else," was what shut him up. He would not risk his safety or that of his family. Refusal was not an option. We still have the title to the property, but I doubt if we will get it back.

I found this to be a reckless way to treat innocent civilians. What an unacceptable way to win the hearts and minds of Filipinos, I thought. Why would the left use the same land-grabbing technique that the oligarchs and wealthy exploited for their own ends? It did not make sense and it made it easier to presume that there was no difference between the sides. What distortions would they make to justify their claims to truth? Were they not concerned about losing their direction in transforming Philippine society? Aside from moral and ethical grounds, any semblance of democracy, or for that matter, any attempt at civil society transformation, dissipated as soon as the movement for social and political change resorted to criminal activities and justified their actions in the name of dissent. In other words, these rebels committed the crimes with the belief that they possessed a higher calling in attempting to transform a capitalist-based society into a more just and equitable socialist society.

Now, many will argue that there is no justification for any crime. To this I agree, though at the time I had little to no inkling that the left behaved so abhorrently during that period. What happened to my family in 1968 was before martial law and, yes, it was true that violence and brutality were common in many parts of the country then. But the land-grabbing incident carried out in our farm happened after Marcos had already left the country and a new government was in power. Their actions planted serious doubts in my mind as to their real intentions and cemented the negative impressions I was beginning to form about them.

For much of that period, there was very little information about the underground movement, unless one made the decision to go up into the hills and join them. The organization was set up as a clandestine operation and by its very nature that meant that information was closely guarded and monitored. The little information that got out to the public rarely depicted them in a positive light. This was the problem for those willing to support their cause.

The left's lack of transparency and its growing penchant for violence was starting to cast doubt about their integrity. The largely untold and unknown directive in which they would take over and present a superior alternative to civil society, in sharp contrast to the dictatorial Marcos regime, remained shrouded in a cloud of secrecy. It was also wearing thin on me. I was deeply disappointed. I still am.

Even so, and in the early days, legions of Filipinos signed on or sympathized with the rebels' cause, an enthusiasm that the movement then exploited to grow its ranks. By the mid-1980s, reports in reputable and scholarly publications were claiming that both the Communist Party and its military arm, the NPA, had grown and expanded in many regions of the country. They extended from Luzon through the Visayas and then spread like wildfire among the Muslim enclaves of Mindanao, where some reports alleged, the CPP had effectively become the de facto local government in villages and towns, where official government rule had collapsed and the army had effectively abandoned these uncontrollable places.

Without a doubt, sentiments against political repression, injustice, lack of economic opportunity, grinding poverty, Philippine-style oligarchic politics, and other social ills, were legitimate justifications for founding the CPP. Filipinos wanted an alternative. But the opacity of an inherently clandestine undertaking left too much room for speculation, untruths, and sometimes, pure fabrication. Marcos exploited their vulnerabilities whenever an opportunity arose. He used his traditional media pulpit to discredit the left with his own brand of truth, knowing full well that the CPP and the NPA would be unable to disavow whatever had been written in the press or announced over the airwaves. He controlled all the media outlets at that point. It was unfortunate that it was these fabrications that filtered down to the general public. For the gullible, these lies were made sufficiently believable. But for those who did not trust the media, who believed that the media was an appendage of the Marcos government, these fabrications proved that the Marcos government would use any means necessary to stay in power.

It was also in these areas—in the avenues of public discourse and in the media marketplace—that shades of gray proliferated. Over time, the deadly cat-and-mouse game between the government and the rebels produced egregious lies, which resulted in consequences that impacted the lives of ordinary Filipinos. Some of these fabrications have now been exposed for the lies and deceptions that they were. But it would be foolish to hold my breath for every single one of these fabrications to be repudiated. Many will continue to be regarded as gospel truth by those who benefited from Marcos' largesse. Or they will simply be buried under the deeply polemical and one-too-many embattled periods of Philippine political history. Many of the characters that played prominently in significant events of those days are still around today. It remains in the interest of the opposing sides to continue to obfuscate the truth.

One of the suppressions by the left is the denial that the CPP and NPA were behind the now infamous Plaza Miranda bombing in 1971. In a third incarnation of Ben Pimentel's book, which is an account of the life of revolutionary and former Ateneo de Manila University student leader, Edgar Jopson, entitled, *U.G An Underground Tale: The Journey of*

Edgar Jopson and the First Quarter Storm Generation,[35] the author provides newly disclosed information claiming that it is entirely possible that the Communist Party ordered the bombing and that Jopson learned about it later and was troubled by the allegation. Similarly, one of the more well known victims of the bombing, Senator Jovito Salonga, in his autobiography, also expressed his belief that the CPP was responsible. The CPP and the NPA, in their current incarnations, have not admitted responsibility and it is possible that they will never acknowledge their guilt. But Plaza Miranda will persist as a significant piece in the history of the country and remains a watershed event in its political history.

It is common knowledge in Philippine society that it was Marxist-leaning students that sowed the initial seeds of dissent and unrest in the 1960s, giving rise to the Communist Party of the Philippines as well as the New People's Army. It was during this period when much of the world watched on as students took to the streets; when they had dialogs in Marxist-Leninist sit-ins and lectures, and attempted to topple the complacent 1950s free market apple cart. By 1969, when Marcos was re-elected for his second term of office, this ragtag band of students, many coming from upper middle class backgrounds, rebel farmers and laborers, chartered the organization known as the CPP. Later, as its membership grew, they formed the NPA.

Like its counterparts in Asia and Latin America, the development of insurgency in the Philippines was initiated first by intellectuals and middle-class radicals

---

35   Pimentel, Benjamin. *U.G. An Underground Tale: The Journey of Edgar Jopson and the First Quarter Storm Generation.* (Pasig City: Anvil Publishing, 2006).

who composed its dogma, offered organizational skills, and sparked the necessary revolutionary zeal. And like the foot soldiers who make up the front lines in combat, the cadres that populated the nascent organization came from the peasant class. Shouts of feudalism, imperialism, and bureaucrat capitalism rang out frequently during student street demonstrations, while the more serious study of Maoist-Leninist doctrine occupied budding revolutionaries in their spare time, away from academic halls and straight into candle or kerosene lamp-lit country huts and mountain hideaways.

Analysis in Western publications about the Philippine insurgency posited that the movement was not taken seriously in its beginning stages. The reason? The West saw the Philippines as very different from the Communist revolutions waged in China, Indochina, and Latin America. It was also based on the country's economic picture from its early days as a fledgling democracy and the supposition that it was a budding economic powerhouse when compared to its poor and ailing Asian neighbors. To take it a step farther, it was argued that the country did not have anything in common with its counterparts in the East except for Japan.

Frankly, I found this idea preposterous. Try explaining this to many who could barely feed themselves and then ask how they saw their lives during that period. Would I have heard the Americans or other Westerners say this about the Philippines when I was living there, I would have told them to come, visit, and then see the predominantly poor people around the country. The country was at that time dominated by rural landscapes, not the urban ones associated with metropolitan cities that signal a bustling economy and growing national wealth. I am certain such a visit would change their minds about the Philippines being a "budding economic power." I would also feel confident that many Filipinos would identify themselves as poor and distinctly aligned with the peasant class. They would also more than likely regard the whole country as poor, especially when compared to the America they looked up to as the epicenter of success and wealth. Many of us never even bothered learning about our neighbors across the borders. We were pretty ignorant about what was happening in the region because our eyes were always looking towards America. We were fixated on a specific prize: We wanted a piece of the American dream. Desperately. This was not surprising given the lack of economic opportunities at home; the fact that the Philippines was a former American colony and many still professed American allegiance; and, coupled with the dominance and influence of American pop culture in every home. Thousands migrated to American shores and many more would leave the country in succeeding years. In this regard, we were easily the unquestioning recipients of American culture and consumers of a vast American free enterprise.

Like many Filipinos, I saw images of poverty at a young age. Sometimes these experiences would hit close to home. I often wondered, for example, why it was that every morning, poor country folks from the rural barrio of Divisoria lined up the door to grandma's house. Our family owned land there and sharecroppers like the ones I saw at grandma's house, regularly borrowed money from her to feed and clothe their children, buy seeds for their crops, or use for their weddings. I always found the scene distasteful, much as I loved grandma. I was none too pleased that she made these people wait for hours, asking them to do things for her around her house before she came around to giving them the money they needed. Later, I was mortified to discover that the loans were provided under an arrangement locally known as "Five-Six," a usurious practice commonly perpetuated in those days by the land-owning class. I was deeply disappointed that a relative would participate in such an inequitable exchange. But the disappointment pales when compared to the fact that many more members of the landowning class made these loans to sharecroppers, which put them in an endless cycle of debt and poverty.

Perhaps it was due to experiencing this scene at grandma's house that I knew quite early the difference between the haves and the have-nots. By the time I was ten years old, I thought it was unfair that I was attending the most prestigious private school in town, while the children of the folks who worked my family's land, would barely finish elementary school. I played with some of these children when grandma took me to Divisoria. I became friendly with them. I would even sometimes teach them things I learned in school and was surprised that they did not know the things I knew. Their mothers were like family to me and they treated us like family too. Yet, despite this closeness, they knew where they stood in terms of social standing.

To add further tension, some of my older relatives looked down on children who went to public schools, many of which were considered inadequate. As my relatives said, "the teachers were not well trained and could not get better jobs and only public schools would hire them." Rather than feeling smug about being a private school kid, I was embarrassed that my family could afford this opportunity. It is no accident then that my sympathies would be invested in those who advocated raising the poor out of poverty.

Sometime during high school, I was introduced to a university student who came to talk about imperialism and feudalism. Her lecture was punctuated by big words I did not understand, though it did not matter. What mattered was that what I would learn would allow me to help the poor, and that was good enough for me.

As a teenager, the only way I could understand the meaning of imperialism was to portray it in simplified terms. I grew up not far from Clark Air Force Base in Angeles City. What I saw there of American servicemen, particularly as they roamed the streets of Angeles, did not do credit to Americans. It was commonly understood that they were out looking for "call girls." At the US Subic Naval Base in Olongapo City, while undergoing bivouac in my high school cadet training required under martial law, I came across some American soldiers drinking and cavorting on the beach, their language so foul and so distressing. These kinds of scenes left a very bad impression on me. It was not just the moral dimension that left a bad taste in my mouth; it was also that I saw the subservience of Filipinos regarding prostitution, or in the local merchants who would do anything to please their free-spending American buyers. I admit that it was these scenes and images that cemented anti-American sentiments in my mind and made me easy prey to the ideas of Maoist-leaning, anti-imperialist zealots.

To be fair, once I enrolled at the Ateneo de Manila University, my American professors, all of them Jesuit priests, taught me far more about social justice than I expected. I admired them greatly. The years I spent at Ateneo stoked my intellectual curiosity. I will not forget that it was they who taught me liberation theology, a kind of theology that grew out of the *fabellas* in Rio de Janeiro. Its dogma resonated among Filipino intellectuals and university students just as it did in Latin America. The same way I was attracted to the lectures on Marxist and socialist concepts, I appreciated what I heard from Jesuits on how religion can potentially be used to understand the dynamics of inequality, injustice, and disenfranchisement of the poor.

I lived not a half hour away from Clark and a mere two hours away from Subic, close enough to see the effects of the Americans on Filipino lives. It was therefore not far-fetched that I would be, as a teenager, against continuing the US bases' placement in the Philippines. Keeping the US bases in the Philippines was one of the most politically contentious issues at the time—hotly debated both in the popular press and in leftist circles. I was sympathetic to the left's insistence that the Philippines got a bad deal as far as the bases were concerned. It was not difficult for me to understand this point of view, given that Clark, with its high fence and tight security, was designed to keep Filipinos out. Dismaying scenes of poor children dressed in rags, rummaging through American garbage, scavenging for metal, plastic or glass bottles that they then sold for a pittance, while being repeatedly shooed away by the base's security guards, were experienced often.

For many of us, Clark was another world. It was definitely not part of the Pampanga I knew or the circles I belonged to. It could not even be considered part of the Philippines despite the country being such a willing and subservient host. The Americans also made it clear that the base was the United States. Yet, when they went out to have fun in the streets of Angeles City, it was to Filipino women they turned to. There were Filipino maids in their homes that took care of their children or cleaned their houses. It was to Filipino guards they hired to secure their homes. I knew personally about the security because one of my uncles owns a security agency in Angeles. A majority of his clients in the 1970s were American military servicemen. To a young and naïve teenager, what was done on these bases and how American soldiers behaved towards Filipinos was imperialism personified. Despite my having gone to private school and my family being landowners for generations, it was difficult for me to consider myself a member of the elite. My family was not very wealthy, even among the standards of wealth in my hometown.

It was a different story when my mother was growing up. My grandmother was a Spanish mestizo, whose father hailed from Spain, sent to the Philippines to become a colonial government official when the islands were a Spanish colony. He owned more lands that he knew what to do with, using the income to finance his opium habit, or so family tales claim. Everyone addressed him as *cabeza*, which means 'head' in Spanish, and with the title, the prestige it gave his family.

His only child, my grandmother, knew intimately what it meant to be part of the mestizo class. According to stories from adult family members, she had gone to school with President Noynoy Aquino's paternal grandmother at the *Instituto de Mujeres* in Manila. Part of the family lore handed down was that Apu Pa was comfortable with her role as a socialite. Even more intriguing was the belief that she didn't spend a lot of time raising her five children herself. We were told that my mother and her sisters each had a nanny to see to their needs so that their mother was free to visit friends or do as she pleased. She was reported to have been away in the summer capital of Baguio enjoying good times with her friends when her husband died of a heart attack. But when my siblings and I were growing up in the 1960s and 1970s, we saw ourselves as middle class, even though Apu Pa continued to socialize with San Fernando's mestizo class.

The political chaos rampant during the 70s when I was a young girl meant we were subjected to the persistent back and forth between the rebels and the military. If you read newspapers or watched TV during the martial law years, it seemed as though the government was winning against the insurgents. But the word of mouth and the books that came out soon after the 1986 People Power Revolution revealed that the NPA had gained traction soon after its establishment in 1969 and had reached its largest membership by the mid-1980s. In one such book, *Inside the Philippine Revolution* by former Washington Post writer, William Chapman, it is claimed that:

> *By 1986, many large areas of the Philippines, like Negros, were affected by the communist guerillas and their converted citizen allies. Begun in the mountains of northeastern Luzon, the insurgency had edged down the archipelago's eastern provinces and had become deeply rooted in many places. It grew most swiftly in the Bicol region south of Manila; in Samar, an impoverished island in the eastern Visayas, and in some islands of the Western Visayas, such as Negros, and Panay. By the time President Ferdinand E. Marcos was deposed, in February 1986, it was known that the NPA was active in sixty-two of the country's seventy-three provinces and that it controlled*

or influenced at least twenty percent of the barangays,
the basic local political units of the Philippines.[36]

To feed their swelling numbers, leftist rebels relied on regular handouts from peasants and gentlemen farmers. The farmers we knew in Pampanga, not surprisingly, did not disclose that they gave the rebels money or food. And we would not have asked. But the stories persisted anyway. I remember wondering if they had asked help from my paternal grandfather, whose farm was in the remote village of Kulubasa. I wondered if they demanded that he provide them a portion of his harvest. And did he acquiesce to their demands? My father never talked about whether Grandpa was approached. Even if he knew, I doubt if he would have told me. This was a difficult subject to broach under martial law, especially given what happened to me in 1973. It was also common knowledge that in exchange for the provisions the dissidents received; they protected villages from the abuses and atrocities committed by the military. This fact was confirmed in Chapman's book, where he writes,

I*t [the NPA] had approximately 20,000 full-time armed guerillas in the field and perhaps half that number in armed militia units formed for local protection.*[37]

It is not an exaggeration to say that peasant folks needed protection from the military. The Armed Forces of the Philippines had, by the mid-1980s, unleashed its brutality

---

36   For a comprehensive account of the rise of the NPA, see Chapman, William. *Inside the Philippine Revolution: The New People's Army and Its Struggle for Power.* (New York: W.W. Norton & Company, 1987).

37   Chapman, *Inside the Philippine Revolution*, page 14.

on the countryside because they suspected that peasants were aiding and abetting the rebels. The military came to be seen as undisciplined, corrupt, abusive, and sometimes regarded as common thieves and ignorant bullies who stole, raped, and killed innocent people. The opposite could not be more true of the rebels that came into their midst in the early years of the underground movement. Their Robin Hood-like personas won them vital support from peasants.

As many of those in the countryside and beyond joined the CPP and the NPA, the organizations' leadership in later years eventually came from the peasant class. Kumander Dante was one. It was a name that everyone knew in the 1970s. He was a mysterious figure, heard about but never seen until his capture in 1976. Stories of his battles with the military abounded; his exploits in the field, though not broadcast in traditional media, were passed around in the "right" circles in San Fernando and beyond. Many accorded him hero status. I even wondered at some point if he was with Olalia when the latter was gunned down in battle. After being hunted by the military for years, his capture was a big achievement for Marcos. Did this mean then that Marcos was winning the war? Did it mean that the movement would now collapse? What did we really know about how many were involved in the underground and how close or how far were they in taking control of the country? These are the questions that we asked. But no one I knew had the answers. The ones that do know were busy fighting in the hills and mountainsides across the Philippines' seven thousand islands.

There was one thing I learned much later about Kumander Dante's capture. I found out about it when I was at TFDP's offices in the winter of 2008. I had called the organization from the U.S. to arrange a meeting with them since I was planning a visit to the Philippines. They said that they had a library that contained much of the information I wanted. When I got there, the librarian warmly welcomed me and gave me full access to their records and library holdings. She even arranged for me to interview an ex-detainee the next afternoon. They had thousands and thousands of pages of reports about political prisoners and the abuses they suffered at the hands of the military. I now possess a copy of a report prepared by a TFDP staff on a visit to Kumander Dante, the alias of Bernabe Buscayno at the military camp and the torture he suffered. The account began.

Bernabe Buscayno was doing social investigation work and helping peasants organize associations and cooperatives in the barrios of Pampanga when he was arrested by government security forces...

He was tortured during and immediately after his arrest and while undergoing interrogation at the CSU-2 headquarters at Camp Olivas. Among the physical punishments he was subjected to were body punching, kicking and jabbing with rifle muzzles, repeated clapping of his ears, pulling and squeezing his scrotum, calculated strangulation squeezing and karate chopping of his throat, cigarette burning of his nape and forearms, squirting the inside of his nose with an intoxicating fluid, manacling of his hands for months on the railing of a bed. He was also repeatedly threatened with death or "salvaging," for refusing to give in to their demands.[38]

38   Quoted from a typewritten report, an internal document of the TFDP, provided to me by a staff of the organization in the winter of 2008.

131

Reading the account made it all so real to me again after all those years. But it also cemented the negative regard I had of the Philippine military. It was worthwhile knowing that I was not wrong about the anger I felt. As validating as it was, here I was, literally facing my demons. They were back. There they were in the dark room with me, rearing their ugly heads once again. I could not breathe; I had to get out. I hastily said my goodbye, mumbling something about returning the following day. Quickly gathering my things, I knew I needed to manage what my body was making me go through again. I got out of the building as quickly as I could. I was almost blinded by the bright sunshine outside after the dark room I was in. I heard a voice telling me to watch my back as I walked towards the corner to hail a taxicab that would take me back to the hotel. Was that a real voice or was it my imagination?

As I sat in the back seat, I was beginning to become undone. But, remarkably, I noticed that the symptoms that I manifested in such circumstances failed to appear this time. I focused on my breath and tried to forget everything else. Moments later, I noticed that my palms were not sweaty and my heart was not beating so wildly. I was relieved to realize that the therapeutic work I had done on this aspect of my life had not been put to waste. I silently thanked the people who had worked with me as the car sped towards the hotel. I continued to focus on my breath, but I could not help feeling distracted because the radio in the car was on and it was loud. The program being aired was a congressional hearing on the alleged corruption of President Gloria Arroyo's husband to the tune of more than $200 million on a broadband network development contract with the Chinese. I could not help but think how some things never change in the Philippines. Corruption will always be a mainstay of political drama. Soon, I was at the hotel, comforted that I was back, but also stronger in the belief that I might just finally be over what had dogged and terrorized me for years.

Given Filipinos' major disappointment with the CPP and the left after the 1986 People Power that drove Marcos out of the country, one begins to wonder how long they intended to wait until taking over the reins of government. Alternately, were they even capable of taking over, given that they lost their chance to do so when Corazon Aquino became president? Many critics believed that the left squandered this opportunity and that internal party struggles had marred the organization. One might even venture to ask: Has dissidence simply become a well-worn career path for budding communists or leftist guerillas? Or some might wonder: have they lost their way, as they increasingly beat a path towards criminality? In their early years, they gave hope to countless masses that joined the leftist fold because Filipinos were in dire need of a political alternative. But the dogma became, over time, increasingly distanced from what was actually happening on the ground. Lives were not getting any better, even for those in areas of the country under the protection of the NPA. Economic statistics from the period, spanning from the late 1960s to the time that Marcos fled the country in 1986, showed that poverty had increased.

While the CPP is not being blamed for the growing poverty since this is as much the fault of Marcos' failed economic policies as well as the unsuccessful intervention measures brought about by international monetary institutions such as the World Bank and the IMF, it indicated that the CPP was too remote and distant to ever truly become a significant factor in the economic and political life of the country. In other words, they had not become a crucial 'player,' specifically not in the way they would be able to influence significant social change, and perhaps not even in any real sense so that the lives of those they purportedly protected would have gotten better after many years of patient waiting.

The left remained outside the mainstream, and while this was deliberate—being seen as 'the other' a pre-determined stance since its inception—many years of armed struggle have only strengthened the government's resolve to extinguish them from existence. Furthermore, the CPP had not made it their mission to put a stop to the oligarchic politics that had been entrenched in the country since independence in 1946. They believed, as Mao did in China, which was the initial model that they adapted, like Castro in Cuba, and then the Sandinistas in Nicaragua, that the struggle must begin in the countryside and from there, fan out to the urban areas of the country.

While some success was achieved in certain areas, I wondered why it is taking so long for the CPP to do the same across the country. Something else must be operating. Over time I have had my own speculations about this but I did not give it the space necessary in my thinking because like many of the experiences I had there, I relegated it to the deep recesses of my mind once I left the Philippines in 1979. It was convenient for me to do that. I needed to block the pain. I needed to live my life in a way that I could ignore the undesirable, the fearful, and the dark side, despite my nagging wish that the country would improve.

Even more important, I was still reeling from the hold the military had on me, despite my being physically released from political detention. For five long years, they monitored my presence by requiring me to report to the camp as if I was on parole. All that was too nerve wracking for me as I moved from being a teenager into adulthood.

By 1986, the people of the Philippines decided they had had enough of Marcos. When they finally took to the streets and drove Marcos away without any bloodshed, it illustrated that the country could instruct the world a lesson or two in overthrowing a despot through peaceful means. Meanwhile, the CPP stayed in the background and Corazon Aquino became president. Much as she was loved, got the mandate to rule the country, and the admiration of the world, her presidency maintained a long-standing political tradition: oligarchic politics was alive and well in the Philippines. The family you came from could well dictate your role in society. Aside from being the widow of slain Benigno Aquino, Jr., President Aquino was a member of the wealthy, land-owning Cojuangco family, a part of the land-owning class that has often times used political power to maintain their economic interests, and, to a considerable degree, expand these assets while in power. Being part of the elite in the Philippines has always meant being privileged both in economic and political terms, with the two never far apart.

Herein lies the difference between the elite in the developing world and those in developed economies. In America, Bill Gates may well be part of the economic elite but it would be wrong to say he is part of the political elite. In the Philippines, the Aquinos were well ensconced in both. This was also true with the Cojuangcos, the Marcoses, the Romualdezes, etc., and the select few oligarchic families that have ruled the country for generations and continue to rule to this day. Then when Gloria Macapagal Arroyo became president, it was not surprising, as she herself is the daughter of a former president, Diosdado Macapagal. Furthermore, Corazon Aquino's son, Benigno III won in the last presidential election in 2010. I am beginning to wonder why the left continues to ignore this destructive pattern in politics. They were asleep at the wheel at the time of the People Power and have remained sleeping now, only to wake up every now and again in order to wreck havoc and violence and show people that they, too, are capable of violence. Now how does that make them different from Marcos or other political leaders?

Returning Home

I heard a couple of lines about rocking around a Christmas tree from a song being sung by a male singer as the massive door of the camp opened. The sound had been coming from a radio in a jeepney that sped down the street, preventing me from catching the next lines of the song. Then I heard another Christmas tune as another jeepney careened past government buildings.

I'd been at the camp for several weeks now. Christmas is approaching. When I walked to father's office yesterday, I noticed the colorful Christmas lights strung along building facades and Christmas trees adorned their entrances. The few private homes on this street were similarly festive. The chilly air that usually came at this time of year had arrived. I wondered if I was going to make it home to celebrate Christmas with my family. I could not help but think about the holiday and how we celebrated it over the years.

Filipinos love Christmas; they love the very idea of it. It is perhaps the most avidly awaited holiday for Catholic Filipinos. It is a time when everyone on the street seems to wear a smile. A time when every kid I knew gleefully anticipated the seemingly endless days of Christmas carols, rice cakes, and other delicacies reserved for the holiday, when their homemade bamboo cannons crackled and boomed from dusk till dawn, and, when hanging their white cotton socks in windows, they wondered if it would be stuffed with cash or a present, and would be doubly happy when it was both. It was the season for adults and children to observe devotions of the nine-day Catholic novena of early morning masses called *simbang bengi*. Or for the more Spanish inclined, *misa de gallo*, so christened because it was the mass said just as the rooster crowed in the wee hours of the morning.

My family was no exception in celebrating Christmas in a big way. I remember it as an endless singing of Christmas songs which stations aired on the radio just as soon as each of the 'ber' months: September, October, November, or December, commenced. I remember the holiday as having a lot of color and lots of food but also plenty of noise. The colorful Christmas lights twinkling in the darkness of night mesmerized me, finding their twinkle reassuring because I was afraid of the dark. I imagined these lights were alive, these joyful souls talking to me, imploring me to be happy too.

I also enjoyed looking at the *parols*, the traditional Christmas lanterns crafted by hometown artisans, which were perched in the front windows of homes. The small ones that hang in private homes were either made of Japanese paper or Capiz seashells. The Japanese paper lanterns were less expensive. Households that could afford it chose the more durable and more complicated Capiz parols, whose shells were cut in various shapes, forms, and sizes, and then dyed in every color and hue. On the eve of Christmas, San Fernando hosted what has become a very popular Christmas lantern festival.

As we walked the crowded streets, my heart would always seem to beat in tandem with the loud music that accompanied the thousands upon thousands of colorful lights emanating from giant Christmas lanterns that sat atop of the trucks that paraded around town for the annual festival. While the different giant parols were displayed around town, we would talk about what we liked and disliked about each entry, all the while wishing that our barrio's own entry would win. The prize was highly coveted and the competition was fierce as every single one of San Fernando's barrios participated and proudly showcased the talents of its artisans. Over the years the festival grew in popularity and became renown across the country. The biblical themes of the parols' designs were the handiwork of local artisans whose skills were passed down from one generation to the next. Years later, the winning entries were sent to be displayed to foreign tourists and other Filipinos at the grounds of the Cultural Center of the Philippines in Manila.

Equally unforgettable were the homemade bamboo cannons, the ones that sometimes got us into trouble with the adults, especially when fingers, bare toes, or other body parts got burned. My siblings and cousins would sneak out of the house when we got wind of plans that other children in the neighborhood were making them to set off as soon as it got dark. We eagerly awaited the crackle and boom the cannons made, clapping our hands over our ears to protect them from the thunderous noise the cannons produced. We watched the glow of the fire from kerosene-fueled torches touching the mouth of the cannon as it traveled down through the bamboo tube, making a hissing sound before it exploded into the air. Our enchantment at seeing the cannons fired again and again would sometimes be dampened by our dismay when a kid got burned as he lit the cannon and it misfired. When children got tired of the cannons, they went back to their homes, ate dinner, and got ready for Christmas caroling. The little bit of cash they received from caroling, they immediately spent buying traditional rice cakes from vendors who lined the main street.

I remember waking up for early morning mass. With sleepy eyes, I would excitedly get ready in the dark and, shivering in the cool December air, walk the short distance to church from my parent's house. Then my family headed back to grandma's house, the roadside already filled with vendors peddling their wares and traditional rice cakes. A wide variety of these cakes and delicacies awaited us: *puto bumbong, tamales, puto lason, bibingka, cuchinta, tibuk-tibuk, kalame,* and more. The bibingka and tamales were my favorites. To make a bibingka, the vendor first spreads the batter on top of a fresh round-cut banana leaf, and when it is almost cooked, the vendor browns the top by covering it with burning charcoal from a metal grill. It is browned to perfection and then sprinkled with freshly grated coconut. The piping hot bibingka, served in brown paper bags warmed our hands, and we would smell its sweet aroma of ground sticky rice batter wafting through the chilly early morning air. Apu Pa never failed to buy the tightly wrapped steamed tamales in banana leaf. Its ground sweet rice flour batter was flavored with chicken broth and coconut cream and then cooked. When it had cooled and congealed, it was molded into squares, wrapped with banana leaf, and topped with bits of roasted meat, bits and pieces of fermented salted duck egg, and a few roasted peanuts, similar to the lotus leaf-wrapped 'Seven Treasures,' offered in Dim Sum restaurants. After being folded, these were tied with a string and steamed. I relished each tamales' flavor and texture. It was pure bliss as it melted in my mouth. We Kapampangans were especially picky about our tamales. My family disdained those prepared by people from other regions. Hands down—home style wins. We'd always felt confident that Kapampangans made food better than any other Filipino.

This feeling of superiority only grew when it came to the specialty foods we made during holidays. Go figure, I thought. Can anyone rival Imang Dandy's tibuk-tibuk: the white creamy-with-a-hint-of-lime-and-vanilla rice cake topped with *latik*, the first pressing of coconut cream that was cooked until it hardened into golden brown, nutty, and crunchy curds? Her nieces and nephews would watch in fascination as the delicacy was churned in huge vats over a fire that blazed in makeshift pits behind grandma's house. It took hours for it to be done to both Apu Pa and Imang Dandy's satisfaction. Wood-and-coconut-shell ladles were used to keep up with the constant stirring. We were fed with the bits and pieces that stuck to the ladles, contentment and satisfaction written all over our young faces as we sat around the fire.

The time-honored visits to Grandma at her Spanish-style ancestral house at Christmas meant partaking in an endless eating ritual, punctuated by offerings of gifts and hugs, followed by a cacophony of excited voices that had savored the culinary delights that Grandma and my aunt had painstakingly prepared. We never failed to complement Imang Dandy after yet another round of smashingly delicious tibuk-tibuk, after filling our stomachs with her exquisite rendition of the typical stew called *sarciado*, or cured meats, cheeses, breads, rice, and other dishes. No one was allowed to leave without sampling at least some of each offering from the Christmas table. The tibuk-tibuk was followed by generous helpings of *leche* flan, a cream caramel custard, and then kalame, a purple yam/sticky rice dessert reserved for Christmas. If we slept over at her house and promised to attend misa de gallo, we would be treated with puto bumbong (purple rice and coconut creamed mixture forced into freshly cut bamboo tubes and then steamed), *cuchinta* (steamed round brown jelly-like rice cakes infused with lye and rosewater), and tamales with our breakfast bought from the vendors lining the street from the church to her house.

Then came Christmas day. The huge spread on the table would include a Chinese-style country ham we called *jamon de chino*, brought home from Manila's Chinatown before Christmas and hung from the kitchen rafters until it was ready to be soaked for twenty-four hours. It was cooked in a marinade of pineapple juice, brown sugar, and spices, and then baked for hours until its skin turned crispy, a taste that combined Spanish and Asian flavors. Next to the warm dinner rolls we called *pan de sal* would be the imported q*ueso de bola*, an Edam-like ball of cheese still encased in its red wax from Holland, reserved for our *Noche Buena* meal. The adults would also have cooked traditional holiday dishes such as *Morcon*, a type of meatloaf but with more of a Spanish influence; chicken *gallantina*, our version of a shepherd's pie; other stews like *asado*, and lots of local sausages we call *longanisa*, that my aunt, who owned a meat shop, would have prepared specially for the occasion. One, of course, would not eat the longanisa without the garlic fried-rice and sliced fresh tomatoes and raw onions or have it stuffed inside a hot pan de sal. All these dishes, cheeses, breads, traditional rice cakes, and desserts would be enjoyed from *Media Noche* (Christmas

Eve midnight) until the night of Christmas day. It was a time we showcased the Spanish and Chinese mix in our family through the foods we ate. It would have pleased my Spanish great grandfather, Canuto Cabral. This was what made Christmas for me as a little girl: family, friends, gifts, and lots of food.

The thought of food was making me hungry, and for the first time since my arrest I felt like eating. I was sitting by the window near the camp's entrance watching jeeps go by and looking at the Christmas lights twinkling on and off, creating a kaleidoscope of colors on the sidewalks. It was already getting dark as I walked back to the conference room. Soon, I thought, Cesar would be here with my dinner. But it was not Cesar who came that evening. It was Ima and one of my older sisters. After the guard brought me to the lobby, I saw my mother and sister standing next to a desk near the toilet. I didn't understand why they would be in that corner of the room as it was very close to the foul-smelling washroom. I was glad to see them but at the same time apprehensive. This was usually the case with family visits. I wanted to see them and be with them and yet I was uneasy about how the scene would unfold. There was a lot that remained unsaid between us. Walking towards them, I took Ima's right hand and kissed it, to show her respect.

"Let's come over here," I told them gesturing in the direction of a spot nearer to the commander's office. "I don't think you would like the smell much in there," I explained, though it occurred to me that there was not much space to entertain them decently anywhere. They would either be near a toilet or near the commander's office, which, I am certain, my mother associated with my arrest.

Ima was wearing her usual St. Joseph's green skirt and blouse outfit. She was a loyal devotee of Saint Joseph because we lived in the San Jose neighborhood. Devotees of St. Joseph always wore the color green that was identified with the saint. Ima used to wear this costume only on Sunday masses and on late Wednesday afternoons, when she went to church for the St. Joseph novena. For the yearly feast of St. Joseph, each March 19, she had our dressmaker create an outfit for her and she celebrated the occasion with a big party for which we would easily entertain a hundred or so guests in the house. I noticed that she wore her St. Joseph's green more often these days.

I greeted my sister and inquired how she was doing. She was wearing a pair of flared pants that were popular in the 70s, not really quite the bell-bottoms that my parents did not approve of, but fashionably wide at the bottom. The pants were dark colored, topped by a psychedelic-patterned blouse of riotous colors, a style that was in vogue at the time. Her shoulder-length hair was resting loose at the top of her shoulders. She wore a leather bag and on her feet were Italian *Famolare* sandals that we loved to wear because the wedged platform heels were the height of fashion. She tried her best to act perky as she greeted me. I could tell that they were uncomfortable and uneasy. I pretended that things were normal.

"You must be quite busy getting things ready for Christmas. Have you been going to early morning mass?" I asked.

"Oh, yes," my sister remarked. "As usual, Grandma has invited the priest and the choir and afterwards we all go to her house for breakfast."

"That's nice. I miss attending early morning mass. And the thought of tamales and bibingka, and hot chocolate is making me hungry," I said.

"Oh, we brought you some," Ima said. "Here." She handed me a basket with its top covered with a kitchen towel.

"Also, we brought your new dress for Christmas. You need to try it on. I brought some pins with me so we can make the proper adjustments. Please hand me the other bag," she instructed my sister.

Ima took the bag from my sister and then gave it to me. I opened it and took out a blouse and skirt, which was decorated with the most beautiful combination of colors I have seen in a long time. It was made of wool, a heavy, nicely woven fabric that looked expensive. It seemed like those tweeds that English people wear in cold weather. The colors were autumnal with woven threads of amber, burnt red, and burnt orange. Very classy—not at all suitable in the room we were in, where the beige-painted walls showed smudges of grime, grease and dirt all over. The handsome fabric and pattern of the Christmas outfit stood in dark contrast to the dimly lit space.

Beauty and ugliness, hand in hand with beauty trying to outsmart the latter.

"What do you think?" Ma asked after handing it to me.

"It's nice," I said without emotion. At that point nothing excited me, even though I really liked the dress.

"What's the matter, don't you like it?" Mom's expression showed disappointment and hurt.

"No, no, it isn't that. It is nice," I quickly replied, adding a little more enthusiasm to my voice. *How can I tell her that I didn't even know if I would have a chance to wear it?*

"Why don't you try it on?" My sister suggested. "We will need to make adjustments anyway and I can put the pins in areas where Indang Soling can see where to adjust." Indang Soling was our dressmaker. She made all our dresses. We could easily have kept her in business all year around with six growing daughters in the family.

I went to the toilet to change, careful not to drop the material on the wet floor. Once I had it on, I looked down to check how it fit me. There was no mirror, so I closed my eyes and began feeling the fabric instead. I ran my fingers delicately up and down, softly touching the fabric to pick up its texture. Its softness comforted me. I was a teenage girl again, joyful and excited about trying on a new outfit. I continued feeling the fabric until my reverie was interrupted by the sound of my mother's voice, right outside the door.

"Is it fine?" she asked, a tinge of anxiety in her voice. She then knocked on the door.

"Yes, it is." I opened the door and stepped out.

"Huh, that's nice, it looks good on you. We just need to make adjustments," Ima said as she fished the pins from a bag and handed some to my sister. The two of them proceeded to put pins here and there on the skirt and then on the top as I stood passively watching them go about their work.

I cannot remember how long they stayed that day. Did we say goodbye? They must have left because I suddenly realized that I was all alone standing in the lobby. I became lost in my thoughts, sadness washing over me. I would have cried but thought quickly that no one must see me cry in this place. I bit my lip, breathed deeply, and then, with resolve, returned to the conference room. I might not be home for Christmas, but there's not much I could do about it.

It is difficult to remember much about what happened days after that. But on the afternoon of Christmas Eve, I was told I was going to be released. I had to sign more forms like I had signed on the day I arrived at the camp. There was something else though; they told me that my release was temporary. I was to report to the camp regularly.

"How often," I asked.

"Oh," said the soldier taking care of the paperwork, "you must come here every other day. The soldier on duty will let you know what to do. Failing to do this will mean you will be sent back not just here but to Camp Olivas."

Luckily, as I was signing the papers, Tang showed up. They must have called him to let them know I was going home. Tang gave me a quick hug, and then talked to the soldiers who informed him of what they had just told me.

Tatang and I exited the building, and headed towards where his government-issued Toyota Land Cruiser was parked. He was silent as we walked together. I looked at him and saw relief etched on his tired face. There was even a quick bounce to his step as we approached the parking area. Ely, his driver, was waiting for us. He told Ely that we could now go home and have a happy Christmas. Ely flashed a big smile and made light conversation as he drove through the gates and turned onto the highway. We drove east towards our neighborhood, which was sandwiched between San Fernando's city center and the town of Mexico. Vendors were selling their wares along the road home. The Land Cruiser continued on past San Fernando's only supermarket at the time, the Essel Supermart, located just across the street from the well-manicured lawn and home of the supermarket's owner. We stopped in traffic at the four-way intersection of the town center. On the same side of the road of San Fernando's only hotel, we waited for the light, inching forward and stopping again in front of the Spanish Colonial cathedral. Across from the cathedral was the municipal hall.

As we waited for the traffic to ease, a little boy pressed his face against the vehicle window. He was dressed in an old, dirty T-shirt and tattered shorts, but his face looked happy. It was the most cheerful face I had seen since the beginning of my incarceration. He smiled and broke out into a song, "*Pascu na, pascu na, nananu co pa?*" (Christmas is here, Christmas is here, what are you waiting for?). Then he stretched his hand, hoping for a coin or two. Every Kapampangan child knew this little tune and sang it for a bit of cash so they could buy candy at the corner store. Tang fished out a coin from his pocket and handed it to the boy. We drove on and soon crossed Highway 54 into the street leading to our house.

After a short drive we turned onto the little side street where our house stood, and then we were home. Tatang called out to Ima and my siblings that we had arrived. Everyone came out to the garage and joined us on the patio next to the kitchen. They all gave me warm smiles and hugs, but after just a few minutes, became quiet. There was an uneasy silence until someone said that it would do me good to go upstairs and rest. "Please do rest," others agreed, "and when you are rested, come down here again for a snack before dinner." *I am being sent away. No one wants to deal with me. Why? Wouldn't they want to know how I am?*

I knew not to ask questions. I was certain that they too were shaken by my having been arrested and branded as a political detainee. And now that it was over, they were all probably thinking: *thank god she's back, and she's not one of those who disappeared. Oh, let's not talk about this. It's too difficult, too anxiety-provoking. Anyway, what's done is done, she's here, isn't she? She's back with us now and that is all that matters.*

That was what it meant to be living under the tight noose of martial law. Rules had changed. We didn't know what was allowed and what wasn't. It all felt arbitrary. We were uncertain how to move on, how to react, how to live so our lives would not be at risk. When one of my siblings or my parents would ask, "*Cumusta na ca?* (How are you?), I soon learned that it meant more than just asking how I really was. Yes, part of the question was to show their concern, to be solicitous of how I was doing. But the other part of the greeting was to convey to me this: I-am-glad-you-are-back-here-with-us-again-but-can-we-just-move-on-from-here-and-not-talk-about-it-anymore. It was also saying to me: gosh, this-is-just-too-agonizing- to-contemplate.

So, on that afternoon of Christmas Eve in 1973, my family began constructing a mask to cover the pain, the fear, and the uncertainty. We also built a wall, an imaginary wall to prevent us from thinking the unthinkable. Finally, we built a cage, an imaginary cage, and wrapped black curtains around it to trap in a monster that had been dropped into our midst. We did not talk about it the next day; no one even asked. Or, for that matter, the next day, or the days that followed, until days turned into weeks, months, and years, and still we never talk about it. Soon the mask, the wall, and the cage grew impregnable, and everyone thought that somehow the monster had disappeared.

I took the family's suggestion to repair upstairs to where my bedroom was. I tried to rest in the room that I shared with my sisters. I sat alone on the bed for a long time. I just sat there, not thinking, not feeling, seemingly lifeless. I did not know what to do next. My eyes saw but I did not perceive. I heard sounds and noises, some chatter here and there, but I did not really hear. I continued to look blankly at nothing in particular. I lay down on the bed even though I was not sleepy. I stared at the ceiling above me until sometime later; I heard a knock on the door. It was our housemaid, Aling, asking me to come down for merienda. I told her I was not hungry. She insisted that I come down. I was at the top of the stairs when I heard mother.

"I heard you, just come down, anyway. Sit in the kitchen with me," she said sweetly as she looked up at me from the bottom of the stairs.

I made my way down. She instructed me to sit at the kitchen table and then put a plate of rice cakes and a steaming cup of *salabat* (ginger tea) in front of me. She cupped both her hands around my face and then looked at me tenderly but didn't say anything. The gesture was enough. I tried to look away. Before the tears came, I said, "I need to go to the bathroom," and walked quickly away from the kitchen.

"Your dress is ready. You'll be able to wear it for Christmas Eve midnight mass," she called out as I was leaving. She knew. She must have sensed my reluctance when she brought it. She, too, was hoping I'd be able to wear it.

Incarceration Trails

A few years ago, I learned of a peculiar Portuguese word: '*saudade.*' It connotes a deep emotional and nostalgic longing for a person, or an object that was lost. Saudade also evokes a fatalistic tone concerning the unspoken knowledge that the object of longing might never return. The Portuguese use saudade to describe a "love that remains," after the person had left, was lost, or died. Its use also encompasses a composite of sentiments, places, or events that elicit joy, excitement, as well as signifying a person's well-being. The word adequately expresses the little provocations that trigger the senses to remember these feelings, thus sparking the longing for "that which is lost." Even more remarkable to me was its reference for a deep yearning, for something that may not even exist, or for that which is unattainable.

I survived that Christmas in 1973. I did not live it; I merely survived. How does one enjoy life again after such an event? How does one re-start life? On the surface, nothing appeared different. The jubilant cheer Filipinos reserved for Christmas still pervaded our town. Homemade bamboo cannons still sounded across neighborhoods. Colorful lights still decorated and lit up the dark at night.

The burnt fragrant smell of bibingka perfumed the air as Christmas caroling woke me up early in the morning or kept me from sleep at night. But something was amiss and I could not figure out what it was. Weeks went by, yet I remained unable to comprehend my reactions to things. Why did seemingly trivial details make me jump out of my skin? Why did I frequently feel besieged one moment—catatonic, dull, and blank the next? The dullness clung inside me, sticking like kudzu. Who was this person I saw in the mirror every morning? Who was this person who was always so anxious to get home as soon as darkness fell? When was the last time she even smiled?

For years after I was released, I was haunted by certain moods and feelings that were unfamiliar, unsettling, and terrifying. I can remember these feelings as alternating between a dull ache and an emptiness followed by a feeling of yearning for something I could not put into words. Then uncertainty would simply take over, like a heavy, black shroud cloaking everything in sight. Sometimes, the uncertainty felt sinister, expressed only by the wild beating of my heart responding to an unknown cause, as though something catastrophic was about to happen. At other times, it felt like a light, lingering uneasiness that was tied up with strands of despair. It felt like how one would react to a rendering of the bleakness of a nuclear winter—you never quite believe it because it has not happened; yet nonetheless, you intuit its radiating hopelessness. And when one no longer perceives the image, all that is left is a lingering blackness.

When I returned to my parents' house that Christmas I noticed a change on the faces of those around me. I also saw it in myself when I looked in the mirror. I experienced it in the moods I displayed. Had I gone crazy? The house, the family, the town—all of these did not give the impression of being different, though something within me sensed that was not the case. A voice nudged at me saying that I could no longer truly go back. *Go back to what? To where? To something that may not have even existed?* It was not until many years later that I learned the word I needed to describe it. I felt saudade.

It was a gloomy, muggy, humid mid-morning as I readied myself to report to the camp. I turned the radio on to my favorite pop music station and heard David Soul singing about not giving up and wishing for another chance with a lover. I couldn't feel the hope that the singer was expressing in song. The sun had refused to come out this morning and it was threatening to rain. The humidity was thickening by the minute. It would only get worse from here, I grumbled to myself. Just another one of those days we normally endured during the hottest months in the tropics. Adding umbrage to my already blackish mental state, the next song to come on was John Denver and his folksy rendition of how sunshine on his shoulders is making him happy.

"Where is the frigging sun," I asked the radio. John Denver makes me sick right now. There is not a bit of sunlight today. *Nada*, and his crooning about sunshine makes me want to hurl the damn radio across the room, and gloat while it smashes against the wall. But this would only get me in trouble with Ima and Tatang.

I got in the shower, my second this morning. Stepping out, I caught Cat Steven's voice crying out the lyrics of *Father and Son*, particularly hitting me when he sang the lines about his needing to have to go away.

Oh yes, if only I could go away. If only I wasn't stuck here in a land where my spirit had run for cover. I could only now see it in fragments—its unity had been shattered. Where was the rest of it?

Oh stop it now, Vicky, Just get on with it. Yeah, I know. But didn't I just go to the camp two days ago? As well as two days before that? And what about the two days previously? How long do I have to do this for? When would it end?

Smack right in the middle of the sticky month of March on a Saturday morning, hoping to enjoy a break from my school books, listening to American pop music on the radio, reading the newspaper or just curling up with a good book; these are the things I wanted. Instead, here I was getting ready to visit the camp. Again. Like the other occasions before today, my stomach was bunching up in knots. Very soon afterwards, I tasted acidic bile coming up from my belly. Its sourness made me pucker. I slowed my pace, took my time getting dressed. When I was done, I sat on the edge of my bed, reluctant to come out of my room. Soon, I heard mother calling from downstairs.

"Do not forget to go to the camp today. Cesar cannot take you as I need him to drive me to the rice mill."

"Ok, ma," I said as I slowly descended the stairs.

"You'll have to take the jeep or calesa," she continued.

"Yes, Ma, I know," I answered. As if I needed reminding, I thought.

I proceeded to walk out of the house towards the jeepney stop at the end of our street. I couldn't make up my mind. *What should I take today? Why couldn't Cesar just drive me? Or anyone, just anyone, please take me there so that I do not have to do this all by myself. Oh, but of course, I couldn't ask Ma. She needed Cesar to drive her to attend to more important matters. I couldn't possibly worry her now, could I?*

I've caused her enough grief as it is. What would she say anyway? Even if she did understand, what could she do? It was what the military ordered, she would say, and that was that.

As I approached the street corner where the jeepney stop was, my heart began to beat faster. A few minutes later and it was beating even more mercilessly against my chest. My palms were sweating so I rubbed them against my blue jeans. I felt the color drain from my face. My nerves added to my indecision about which transport to take. Maybe, the jeepney would do. Or else the calesa?

I waited anxiously for a jeep that would take me. Minute by ticking minute, my dread increased, filling up every bit of space in my stomach and was spreading to other parts of my body. I tried to amuse myself by thinking irreverent, unkind thoughts about drivers and their jeepneys.

The jeepney is a uniquely Filipino people-ferrying vehicle, often packed to the roof with passengers, animals, and whatever else needs transport. It was called 'jeepney' after the U.S. military jeep, an American relic of the Second World War, retrofitted by the natives. It had become the cheapest and the most popular means of public transportation across the country, even in remote barrios that were coming into their own and dispensing with wagons and carts pulled by the omnipresent carabao, a type of water buffalo.

Jeepneys came in various sizes, colors, and designs, physically far removed from the original look of its combat-green American progenitor. The body of the vehicle is often found painted in vivid reds, blues, greens, yellows, purples, or other bold colors and then adorned with graphic designs suited to the prosaic tastes of jeepney drivers. Drivers often owned their jeepneys and decorated them in a style I could only describe as an attempt to smother all good taste. Colegialas had slang for this: *bana*. I am not certain if the word is a corruption of the word 'banal,' but its meaning comes close. In those days, even as I began to reject the trappings of exclusive private school culture, I had not yet learned to inoculate myself against the lingo affected by colegialas and I was guilty as anyone in my school of upper class pretensions. But in the matter of the jeepney, the gaudier the style, the more the driver seemed to like it. His jarring use of juxtapositions between the religious and the secular resulted in an artistic imprint that can only be described as garish, or to Catholic sensibilities, disrespectful. What possessed these men to embellish their vehicles in this manner? It astonished my convent school upbringing how jeepney drivers would see nothing wrong in putting religious icons next to images of scantily clad women. Kapampangans, at least the ones I saw growing up, were predominantly a Catholic and religious lot. Churches were always packed on Sundays. But along with their church going ways, jeepney drivers frequented top bars or the nightclubs euphemistically called *kabaret*, where they could procure women for a price. Another word I often heard, as a child was "*querida*," the Spanish word used to refer to a lover, usually the 'other woman' in an illicit affair. Despite their meager earnings, Jeepney drivers were some of the worst offenders of the querida culture. It was a macho side of the culture carried over from the chauvinistic inclinations of Spanish colonial rule.

Many jeepneys passed me by, too full to take any more passengers and ridiculously packed not only with people, but with caged chickens riding its roof. Soon, another slowed down. The driver asked if I wanted to squeeze into whatever few inches were left on the bench-like passenger seat.

"No thanks," I said and shook my head.

As he drove away, I noticed that his jeepney was painted with vivid red pictures of come-hither type women in bikinis. Moments later, another one stopped. This too was packed. Two passengers were even sitting on the floor. The driver gave me a wee smile; like he was disappointed he was unable to squeeze me in. The jeep's body was a mere inch or two from the road. It would scrape the ground if he did not drive slowly. As I checked out the scene in his jeepney, I took it that the driver might be religious. His jeepney was adorned with several rosaries dangling from the rear-view mirror and emblazoned along the inner sides of the roof were the beginning words of the Lord's Prayer in Tagalog, "*Ama namin, sumasalangit ka....*" (Our father who art in heaven....)

Where was the godly father when I needed him?

The dashboard was crammed with religious figures of popular saints like St. Christopher, the patron saint of travelers; St. Joseph, always attired in his green robe and holding a lily, and then there was the Sacred Heart of Jesus, easily distinguishable by the blazing heart on his chest.

Tilting my head towards the direction of town, the silhouette of a calesa was beginning to take shape in the distance. Maybe I would just take the calesa. The calesa is a horse-drawn carriage that dates back from Spanish colonial times, roughly between three and four hundred years ago. It refuses to relegate to the past in San Fernando and has remained a viable means of human transport. It is still being used to this day despite San Fernando having evolved into a city, bustling with all kinds of cars, trucks, vans and other vehicles. But we Kapampangans are a traditional lot. Seeing the calesa clip-clippity clopping its way into the crowded streets is a constant reminder of a past we won't give up.

The jeepney won out when one stopped and had enough space for me. It would be faster, I thought. I braced myself for the jostling as the vehicle suddenly braked and then lurched jerkily throughout the duration of the trip. I tolerated the hot, smelly, and uncomfortable ride because it was fast. The quicker I got this done, the better I would feel. I held my breath intermittently while inside the jeepney as body odor from a passenger or two wafted across the confined space. I did not mind having to rub shoulders with people, as they provided cover for me. I would be inconspicuous, at least until I got to the camp. Maybe the man I saw the other day who I thought was following me would not be able to tell which jeepney I was riding in today.

Half an hour later, I reached the camp. As I got out of the jeepney, the familiar sight of the entrance with a camouflage-wearing guard standing on duty by the gate, greeted me. I had seen this sight so many times before, yet I could not get accustomed to it. The short, squat, and dark–skinned guard, who looked interchangeable with all the others, gave me a quick nod.

"Don't bother going in," he instructed. "I've got the ledger right here." He reached down into the shelf of a wooden podium in front of him and pulled out the gray cloth-bound logbook. The logbook had become a familiar sight by now, with its inch-thick pages painted red on the side. The guard opened it slowly. I did not say anything. He and I knew what needed to be done. I waited patiently, making sure I followed his instructions. I never knew with this particular guy. Sometimes he was friendly.

Sometimes he had an angry look on his face. I did not care to remember his name. He was just someone who ordered me to sign my name in the logbook, I told myself. Nothing more. As far as I was concerned, he ceased to be a part of my life once I was outside the gate. I continued to wait until the guard was good and ready. I did not want him screaming at me just because he could.

On the lined pages, he scrawled the day's date. This was a new page. As he turned to the blank page, I glanced at the one before it. It was already full of the names and signatures of those who came before me today. He marked the line where he wanted me to sign with a little red check at the margin. I wrote my name and he scribbled his own signature next to mine. Now the deed was done. He and I knew that at this time and on this date, I was here. That was all the military needed of me. The thing that assured them that I had not run away to the mountains of the Sierra Madre or elsewhere in the foothills and jungles of Central Luzon and joined the subversives.

He snapped the book shut. In a voice I knew well by now he said,

"See you day after tomorrow." He never failed to say this in a tone that was intended to intimidate me, as though he was really saying, *don't even think of not showing up here, understand?*

I walked away without looking back, thankful the ritual of the day was over. Ambling towards the jeepney stop for the ride back home, I sighed. *Whew! Nothing happened to me today.* I looked around and did not see anyone following me. But yet, as with every other day that I reported at the camp, it felt like I had just gone through a kind of death. I was relieved when a jeepney showed up not long after I arrived at the stand.

The relief I felt also had its own sort of procedure. Only when the terrible beating of my heart slowed to a more regular rhythm, and my palms stopped sweating did I begin to feel angry, angry at these men about what they made me do every other day. I would then imagine having a conversation with an army general. Or in my more wicked moments, I imagined it was Marcos himself who stood in front of me to ask if I had been obeying his order. And when he would ask me if I had been good about reporting to the camp, I would say the lines that I rehearsed in my mind over and over again:

> *I swear to you that I, Maria Victoria Pinpin, was here in the military camp, present, with all my faculties intact, hoping and praying not to go crazy, paying homage to you even though I feel like dying when I do. I have signed before your soldier, at this time in the morning or afternoon on this day and it would please you to know that I am nowhere near the mountains where insurgents are alive and kicking the hell out of you....*

I finally surrendered to the rage I reserved for these men. As far as I was concerned, these men were nothing more than bullies and murderers. By giving in to the rage, I sensed a little bit of my old self, the one who did not cower in fear. It was a mental conversation I relished because it seemed the only thing left for me to do.

For the two years following my release, I was required to report every other day. The only concession given was when there was a major holiday, the camp would be closed, and they would instruct me to report on the first day that the camp was open again. Then my probation was reduced to one visit a week and then, much later to once every two weeks. At the fourth and fifth year, it had become once a month. After five long years, I was given a permanent release order, on which I saw that I was identified as Detainee Number 3229, a detail that showed prominently at the top of the page, pronouncing that I had simply become a number.

I learned years later that my father had worked hard to ensure that I had a fully written order of my permanent release as a political prisoner. Tatang never once mentioned this to me; he simply did it. That was the kind of person he was. I wonder to this day what was going through his mind as he navigated his way through the labyrinthine military establishment, seeking out who could best help him and they, the military, giving him the runaround. I asked myself what he thought of torture since everyone knew what was going on at the camps. I wonder what it was like for him to talk to the military powers at Camps Crame, Bicutan, Bonifacio or wherever these high ranking military men may be. I wonder what arguments he chose to lobby the release of his daughter from their clutches. But alas, I could only wonder, since this subject has long been hidden behind a mask, with walls and a cage we built around it. The only thing that my older sister, C., could tell me was that Tatang wanted to make sure that I was not going to have any problems should I opt to go overseas. I think that was his secret wish for me.

The matter of safety and security for one's own person was rarely guaranteed in a place like the Philippines. Settling scores by killing suggested that human life was cheap. What I had witnessed—hearing gunshots yards away from where I sat at my aunt's grocery story when I was ten and seeing the bloodied torso of a man in the back of a green station wagon minutes later; the regular sounds of gunshots of private armies and goons of local politicians; or the string of political killings committed both by the government and by the left under martial law—were indications of the lack of value for human life.

Life was cheap because there were those who were only interested in protecting their own interests and not that of the nation. Life was cheap because many paid lip service to the rule of law but thumbed their noses when it came to professing genuine commitment to its implementation. Sure, we had laws. But no law would amount to a hill of beans, as they say, if people did not obey them. But in the 1970s, not even politicians who enacted these laws cared. In fact, in more than a few cases, they were its worst offenders. Even more distressing, those who committed violent acts were seldom punished. For many years, international organizations such as Amnesty International considered the Philippines a place where the government had, over time, "failed to fulfill its obligation to protect the right to life of every individual in its jurisdiction."[39]

This dismal failure resulted in a culture of impunity with a serious and corrosive effect on both the individual and collective psyche. I was no exception. It took me years even just to comprehend the state of my psychological disequilibrium. To this day, I experience an uncomfortable visceral awareness each time I try to recall how my detention has wrecked havoc on my young life. Intrusions into my private life were some of the events that dogged me countless times. I knew without a doubt that I was

---

39   The pattern of extrajudicial killings did not stop even as Marcos exited from political power and fled the country. This is detailed in many reports by international human rights organizations. See for example a 2006 report by Amnesty International entitled, *Philippines: Political Killings, Human Rights and the Peace Process.* Available online at http://www.losangelesemploymentlawyer.com/SDSHHH-and-the-Harvard-Human-Rights-Clinic-Submit-Evidence-of-Torture-to-the-UN-Special-Rapporteur-on-Torture-PDF/Appendix-C-Amnesty-International-Philippines.pdf.

being followed, for instance. Even if nothing happened, it always felt like I was being stuffed inside the trunk of a car where everything around me was pitch black and I could hardly breathe. Lack of assurance of my safety was an ever-constant threat.

It was a special day in mid-March, the feast day of St. Joseph. In our neighborhood, every household was cooking up a storm, with everyone inviting friends and family relations to celebrate. The main street was clogged, as was the neighborhood church where masses were held hourly in honor of the saint.

As a St. Joseph devotee, Ima was even keener than most to make it a big day, and we were expecting a large crowd at home. She hired an extra cook and helpers for the occasion, though she herself preferred to do the food shopping so that she could choose the freshest ingredients. On this particular feast day, she asked me to go with her to the local market.

Ma and I arrived at the wet market during peak shopping time: large crowds, lots of noise, and lots of pushing and shoving. Vendors were out in full force selling tropical fruits, native vegetables, and flowers. Others were selling little trinkets and toys. The market was located west of the town's main plaza and was constructed of heavy steel beams painted a barn-red color, topped with a corrugated roof that collected all the heat from the blazing sun. Being inside meant you would sweat. Exiting it meant that you smelled like the market. Though the foundation was laid with concrete masonry, its floors were always wet and muddy; dirt mixed in with the detritus of produce that had been ground to a pulp under hundreds of feet. Butcher stalls lined one side of the market, with slabs of pork and beef dangling from iron hooks above huge wooden butcher blocks. There, buyers chose the part they wanted and asked the butcher to carve the meat, depending on how it would be cooked. The live chicken vendors were lined in another part of the market with the chickens in metal mesh cages behind them. The buyer would choose a live chicken from the cages and it would be killed and dressed while you waited. If you did not want to wait, you could go to the fruit and vegetable vendors sandwiched between the meat and chicken stalls.

Ma and I jostled with the crowd, she being a few inches ahead of me. When we were in step together, she looked at me and asked, "Are you okay? You look quite pale." She took my hand in hers.

"Oh I'm alright. It's the heat and the smell. I am hot." I lied. I did not want her to know that I thought I saw someone following me. Besides I was not sure, so why bother her about it.

"We'll be out of here soon, I just need to pick up a few more items," she said.

As we walked, we were accosted by the smells of fresh meat, the sweet fragrance of tropical fruits, as well as the previous day's produce left to rot and stink alongside the muddy canals surrounding the building. Vendors shouted at the top of their lungs, peddling their wares. They desperately tried to get our attention by waving their arms, asking us to come see what they had on offer. A few even touched my arm, a gesture that made me even more uncomfortable. The cacophony of sound, smell, and brash physical movement of people was an assault on the senses if one was not used to this frenzied chaos on a market day.

As Ma and I pushed our way forward with the crowd, I saw a man looking at me. He was not very tall, and had longish, wavy black hair, and a dark face that looked only darker against the white shirt and dark gray pants he was wearing. Something told me that he has been watching me for some time. Was he the same man at the military camp, one of the soldiers, only dressed in civilian clothes for now? I began to feel tense. I looked down, bending my knees slightly, hoping that by doing so I would look smaller and hopefully inconspicuous in the crowd. I looked up every now and then hoping to see if the man was carrying a gun. I could not tell. He was not going to shoot me in the chaos of the market, was he? I edged myself closer to my mother and that was when she asked if I was okay. After I answered her, I decided to walk faster.

"*Capamu, capamu. Eca mamalagwa,*" (Wait, wait, don't be in a rush) Ma chided. I complied but remained uneasy. I could feel beads of perspiration dot my forehead and drip down my cheeks. My palms were starting to perspire. I looked up again. The man was still looking at me. He was holding a cigarette, put it in his mouth, inhaling deeply. My heart began to race. Ma did not notice that I was restless as she stopped at fruit and vegetable stalls to fill the two baskets I carried. I looked down again and did not look up until we were close to the opposite end of the market. We soon made our way back to where Cesar was parked. I could not wait to get inside the vehicle because my knees were wobbly. I was relieved when I finally plopped myself onto the back seat. I crossed my arms around my chest, feeling cold, despite the humid heat. My skin felt clammy. Then I uncrossed my arms and laid my hands on my knees, which were beginning to shake. I knew a headache would soon come. I looked behind me and could no longer see the man. I couldn't erase the image of how the man was looking at me with such intensity. When we got home, I asked to be excused and rushed upstairs to my room. I knew I had to nurse the violent headache that always came after incidents like these.

A similar incident occurred when I was in my freshman year at college in Manila. I was then living with two of my sisters in a dormitory run by Salesian nuns. The dorm was located on United Nations Avenue, close to the regional headquarters of the World Health Organization and west of the city hall, not far from the college. Like many students, I took the jeepney to and from classes. The jeepney routed to take me to the college did not run along UN Avenue, so I had to walk four or five blocks to pick it up.

One afternoon, after all my classes were completed for the day, I took the jeepney, disembarked at my usual stop and began the walk back to the dorm. It was already late in the afternoon and dusk was falling. I was looking straight ahead when I sensed someone was watching me. I turned around and saw a man wearing black pants, a white shirt, and a cigarette dangling from his mouth. As soon as I saw him, he turned away, like he did not want me to know that he was observing me. I continued walking, but that stretch of the sidewalk had very few people on it, so I became a little apprehensive. I quickened my pace and decided to cross the street. A few minutes after I did, the man followed me, and he was now about a hundred yards or so behind me. I pretended that I did not see him and tried to act normal. It was getting darker despite the streetlights. I was afraid the man would grab me right there. I crossed the street one more time just to see if he was indeed following me. He did. Then it occurred to me that the man was vaguely familiar. I snuck another look over my shoulder. Sure enough, I recognized him. He was the same man who had been watching me at the market.

I started to run the rest of the way and did not stop until I saw the entrance of the dorm where the security guard stood at the lobby. I darted inside as quickly as I could and bolted the few steps across the courtyard leading to the dorm building. I sat on one of the couches by the front desk to catch my breath, waiting to see if the man would follow me all the way to the dorm. He didn't, so after a few more minutes, I began climbing the stairs to my room on the third floor. My hands had stopped sweating but my skin was still clammy. A violent headache soon followed.

When these things happened, I never knew whether to believe that what I saw was real or if I was just getting myself all worked up for nothing. Then I would tell myself that I did see the same man following me. I did not know what to do about it; if I waited long enough, and pretended it did not happen, it would go away. I distracted myself with school, books, and sometimes movies. But one thing I never did was to tell my family about it. Maybe I did not want them to worry. Maybe I wanted to think that we were over what we went through during my incarceration and was avoiding every big or little thing that would remind them of it. I knew instinctively that my being followed was related to my arrest and that was probably why I was more than careful not to let anyone know. I felt that I had burdened them enough already.

During my first year at university, I took a course in theater production. One of the final requirements was to stage a play with other students, all of us producing, directing, and staging the performance. The plays were to be performed in the college auditorium and Mr. D., our professor, had encouraged us to invite as many people as possible to watch, scheduled one night before final examinations week. My team had chosen to produce and stage a play that was a parody on Philippine politics. The play revolved around a beauty pageant and each of the characters was a caricature of those in political office at the time. I don't know why no one bothered to ask if this was acceptable to the censors since, after all, we were still under martial law. But even our professor thought nothing of it. So after several weeks of preparation and rehearsals, we were ready for the performance.

There were going to be four plays staged that evening and we would be the third group to perform. In the middle of the second play, I saw three soldiers in combat fatigues enter the auditorium. We were seated in the auditorium since the production crew of the second play occupied the backstage. The three soldiers approached the Dean of Students of the college. She remained in her seat, but a few minutes later, walked over to Prof. D., who was seated in the front row, not far from her. I felt that something was up but would not know for sure until we were about to begin our own performance. Our group assembled at the backstage area but as we were about to begin, the Dean stood up and approached the stage. She said that she had an announcement to make. Due to unforeseen circumstances, she said, the third play, which was our play, was not going to be shown that evening. We would now move on to the last play, she stated. All the members of our production team looked at each other and everyone started talking at the same time. We intuited that the soldiers had something to do with the announcement. After the performance of the last play, we quickly sought out Prof. D. and asked him. He said he was as baffled as we were. I could not tell if he was telling the truth or if he was keeping something from us, but I understood that we were to obey what the military ordered. I have no idea to this day how the military knew about the play. The college that I attended at the time was a small liberal arts college and was not the kind of place that was associated with the student demonstrations and rallies that occurred in major state universities at that time. In fact, this was the reason my father wanted me there and not at any of the larger universities. The following year, my disenchantment with the college's lackluster academic standard prompted me to transfer to the Jesuit-run Ateneo de Manila University.

But that night, after a little get-together with our group to commiserate with each other over the disappointment at being forbidden from performing something we had worked so hard on, I decided to take a taxi to come home instead of the usual jeepney. When I saw the soldiers earlier that evening, I thought I was going to be in trouble again and did not want to take a chance by walking back to the dorm from the jeepney stop. The fear stayed with me for some time, accompanied by a headache that dogged me through the rest of that night.

In early January of 1974, right after observant Catholic Filipinos celebrated the Feast of the Three Kings, I returned to school at St. Scholastica's Academy. One morning, I was standing alone in the hallway right outside the classrooms, looking out toward the main courtyard. As usual, I was dressed in the school uniform, a starched and ironed indigo blue Indian cotton jumper with a white ruffled cotton blouse, white cotton socks, and black leather shoes. A round embroidered letter J was sewn on the right strap of my jumper, indicating that I was in my junior year of high school. In front of me was a four-foot concrete railing. It was mid-morning recess and I was staring out into the open space below without looking at anything in particular. It seemed I was the only person around. No, in fact, it seemed like I was the only person left on earth. I was not lonely, not really, but I was alone. The usual noises I associated with school: girls screaming while playing in the school yard, a teacher blowing a whistle amidst the din of courtyard noise, the metal seesaws creaking as they heaved up and down, as well as the occasional sound of cars and trucks driving along Highway 54—all were silent, though not for long. I was only imagining the silence.

Once I woke from this reverie, the usual noises continued. As I gazed out into the distance, I felt a gentle tap on my shoulder. I turned around and found myself face to face with Ms. C., one of the teachers assigned to teach junior year students. I had always liked her. She gave me a sweet smile, her face lighting up, an expression that I had come to associate with her. She fixed her eyes on me with tenderness that took me aback. I had not seen kindness like that at school directed towards me in a long time. She was about to say something but hesitated. She looked around. She waited as one student and then another passed along the hallway. And when she was certain that no one was around, she put her hand lightly on my arm and said,

"Vicky, I just want to welcome you back. I am very proud of you. You did a brave thing. If there's anything I can do to help you catch up with schoolwork, or with anything, please let me know." I looked at her, not quite believing what she was saying.

"Thank you," I said softly, feeling a lump forming in my throat. My heart began to race as I realized that someone at the school had dared talk to me. As she walked away, those few seconds of conversation relieved me from the suffocating emptiness that had laid claim on me more times than I could count. I recognized at that moment what I had been feeling since I went back to school. No one wanted to talk to me, except for a few words, but not really the kind of talking that I needed. No one seemed to pay me any attention. The students and teachers at my school acted as if I was without a face, someone who did not matter. Yet, as I heard the words that Ms. C. uttered, something started to claw its way back to where it belonged. It was fleeting but it was enough to gain a glimpse of the self I had lost. I savored this tiny slice of time when I forgot the fear. I forgot the informers rumored to be at school. I forgot to be on guard. I forgot the strange looks I got when I returned to school after my arrest. I forgot the silence bestowed by the school friends I thought I had. And Ms. C. thought I was courageous. I thought she did a heroic thing in speaking to me, compromising her own safety.

For years, my having been sent to prison seemed to be the only reality left. As it turned out, it was actually the only reality left for those around me. It was the first thing that relatives said about me to other relatives who we had not seen for a while: "Don't you remember, this is Vicky." "*Yapin ya ing mekulong. Itang aktibista.*" (She was the one put behind bars. She's the activist.) "*Ha, yapin ya ine?*" (Oh, she is the one, is she?) The other person would reply and then they would look at each other and then at me like they could not believe that they actually knew someone who was sent to prison. Surprise and mortification soon filled their faces. By then I would visualize myself slithering away until I could just melt or disappear into thin air. I would yet again suffer another dying.

It was the same thing for those old and forgetful relatives, like my grandfather who had trouble remembering who anyone was. We rarely saw him when we were growing up because he lived in a farm far from town. Ingkong Ando, as we called grandfather, belonged to a different era, one where men always wore hats and carried their gentleman's cane every time they left the house. They were meticulous about the way they dressed, hair neatly in place, pants and shirts always ironed, and a white handkerchief in their pockets.

One day, grandfather came to visit. As each child kissed the back of his hand as a sign of respect, he asked who the child was. Each child announced his or her name and then it was my turn.

"*Ninu ica*," (Who are you?) he asked me as his stooped shoulders and slightly bent body turned in my direction. His eyes squinted as he looked at me.

"*I Vicky pu ini*," (I'm Vicky, sir) I answered formally as I lightly kissed the back of his hand. Maintaining his quizzical look, he was still trying to place who I was when mother stepped in and said,

"Father, she's my seventh child. Don't you remember her? She was the youngest for quite a long time," mother explained.

Grandfather remained confused and then began saying my name over and over again to no one in particular. A few minutes later, his eyes lit up as he said,

"Oh yes, I remember now. She was the one, who was sent to jail, isn't she? She's your activist daughter. The radical."

My mother and I looked at each other. My grandfather and I had this same conversation three months ago when we saw him at Christmas. He said the exact same thing.

He did not remember. But he remembers me for the one thing that everyone else remembers about me.

The times when I sensed that the person I was talking to had malicious intentions were worse. I remember an aunt—she thought that she was always right; and she painted herself as being not only beautiful but also smart. Because she thought these things about herself, she believed she could do no wrong. Family relations learned not to cross her. You couldn't win, everyone said. Nor did she care if she hurt others with her insensitive remarks. I remember a particular incident at a party at her house when she was introducing me to her friends and office colleagues. She walked me around the room with her arm wrapped in mine like a sling, like I was an object she was showing off for everyone to gawk at. She said to her guests,

"This is my niece who was arrested. She's the activist. *Matapang ya iyan.*" (Meaning she's tough or brave but with the knowing look she gave her friends: she's a bitch, if you get my drift.)

She kept saying the same thing to every person she introduced me to. And when she uttered the word, 'activist,' it sounded pejorative because she intended it to mean that I was different, that I rejected our trait of keeping group harmony, what we call "*pakikisama.*" That I deliberately did not tow the line and so must suffer for it.

And so on it went.

"Oh, she's the one, huh? Now, I remember, when was she arrested again?" And of course the other person would then relate the details as if I wasn't there. "She was the one taken by soldiers at her school." That was another conversation starter. And then the person, without sensing that I was squirming away, would face and ask me, "So what did you really do that they had to arrest you?" There

I would just simply say I didn't know and shut up, hoping that interest in the subject would wane. How could I make this person understand when he or she had already condemned me before I'd even opened my mouth? How could I make this person see that my story was the story of countless others in the country and that we were all going through a difficult period in our lives?

Sometimes they used the word 'arrested.' Other times they said, 'sent to jail.' And still other times it was "*meracap*," which in Kapampangan means, you were caught, though it has a worse connotation because it implies that one was fleeing and was caught in the midst of escape.

How could I explain that all I was doing was sitting in school that morning, listening to the teacher and not running from gun-toting soldiers? For these relatives and friends, the one thing they chose to retain about me was that I was 'the one'—jailed, arrested, taken by soldiers at school, or incarcerated—the words they used didn't matter. It did not even matter to whom they said it to; nor did it matter that I was right there to hear it all. At that point, I ceased to be a teenaged girl, a convent-school girl. I ceased to be the seventh child of my parents. I ceased to be the sister to eleven other siblings. I ceased to be a cousin, a niece, a granddaughter to an ever-growing family of extended relations. I even ceased to be my name. I simply became the 'one who was sent to prison.' It represented the whole of me like a scarlet letter sewn onto my chest.

It was a similar story at school. The silent treatment I received from both students and teachers when I returned after my arrest was a testament to how things changed. In my young girl's heart, I wished that the people at school were more like Ms. C. I wished that they could have just uttered a kind word here or there. I wished that they could have welcomed me back even for courtesy sake.

I was so full of shame that I began to see myself as a troublemaker. I blamed myself for having the knack to rock the boat. I considered myself a selfish and angry teenager who thought only of herself and not of others, as I had been instructed by my German-nun teachers. I could already see Sister Celsa, my favorite teacher from second grade, looking at me now with her sad blue eyes and, who passed away by the time I was in high school. I had been her favorite back then. But now I had brought shame not only to my family but also to my school. I wished the nuns at St. Scholastica's Academy were more understanding, more forgiving. But none of them said anything to me. In their habits, frequently with rosaries in their hands, where is their love now? There was only silence.

The reality of my arrest was the one and only thing that stood between them and me. Sure, they wanted to cover their backs too. I understood that. But it also provoked in me resentment about Catholicism that I had not felt before. I knew then that the seeds of doubt about my religion had been planted.

Those around me did not know that each encounter, verbal or otherwise, felt like death. These encounters felt like a thousand little deaths thrown like darts piercing me bit by bit, hitting some part of my body, but never quite striking the deathblow. Each time an insensitive remark was uttered from their lips, another dart was thrown my way. By the time their sentence was completed, my face would have turned red and hot. I would feel myself getting smaller and smaller until I wished that the earth below would just swallow me.

Let me be clear about one thing: the word 'aktibista,' or activist, was not always derogatory, in the way my aunt or others used it. For many enlightened citizens, the word was applied to those worthy of a badge of honor; meaning that one was courageous enough to stand for principles, or that one was willing to go against the grain for things that truly mattered. Being an activist was closer to being a hero because you had put your life on the line. And so for those who believed in Marcos and thus had faith in his government, being an activist meant being a rabble-rouser, a troublemaker, or worse, a nihilist. For those who were disenchanted with the country's state of affairs, activists or radicals were necessary in summoning what little opposition Filipinos could muster against the coercive power of Marcos and his men.

I discovered many years later just who some of these other activists were. It was gratifying to know that one of them was a beloved member of my family. My older sister, C., was then a student at the state university. She disclosed to me in one of our conversations that when she was told by our parents that I had been arrested, her first thought was, why not me too? There she was, a student involved in demonstrations and sit-ins supporting social justice, with other activists and student leaders and yet she was not arrested. She believed that being sent to jail in those days was a step closer to being a hero, because by doing so you indisputably placed yourself on the other side, on the left, on the side of the downtrodden and the oppressed. "Besides," she intoned in her older sister voice, "I could endure it better than you could because, let's face it, you were only fifteen and much too young."

So life went on, with its ups and downs and in-betweens. Sometimes, the pressure got intense. Martial law continued and so did our fears and our anxieties. Despite these pressures, I sometimes found myself giving in to the silliness, the farce, the tragi-comedy of the Marcos years. A particular incident that I can remember even now with a smile was one of those elections that Marcos seemed to always be holding. Marcos was fond of elections. He called for elections even when these were not scheduled. It was as if by doing so, he could tell people he had won and had the mandate, even if his men had stuffed the ballot boxes.

I was sixteen when Marcos called for another election. We all knew what this meant. As preparations were underway, he thought he would at least give it a semblance of legitimacy by allowing the opposition to participate. But stuffing ballots would again win the day; that was how it has been and the way it would be for this election. Even more important he dropped the voting age to fifteen from twenty-one. He also declared that voting would be mandatory and those who did not vote would go to jail. My siblings and cousins, who were fifteen and over, were incredulous that we could vote in a presidential election. We began talking about who we would vote for since there was really no choice about abstaining.

I raised my hand immediately amid the clamor at Grandma's house where we were assembled.

"I know who I will vote for," I volunteered.

"Who," they asked. "Surely not Marcos?"

"Are you serious?" I retorted.

"Knowing you, you would never vote for him," they agreed.

"Well, since this is just a mockery of an election, I will

vote for Mickey Mouse," I declared. 'Mickey Mouse money' was what we called paper money when we played house as kids.

"Maybe I can vote for Donald Duck," someone said.

"Would you vote for Dolphy?" A cousin inquired.

"Why not, he is probably more popular than Marcos." Dolphy was then the country's most popular comedian.

And so it went, each one in the group saying whom they would vote for. On Election Day, I promptly walked to the elementary school in front of our house to cast my ballot. After I drew the booth curtain closed, I looked at the ballot and saw that there was a space to write in a candidate. In handwriting that I deliberately made squiggly and child-like, as if I was just learning to write, I wrote Mickey Mouse. Maybe they would think a little child wrote it, I thought. That's good, that's good, I said to myself. How about that? Mickey Mouse has just been voted as President of the Philippines. He had at least one vote and I would not have been surprised if my many cousins also wrote down his name. Viva Mickey Mouse!

I still did not have a name for the dull ache that had now become an inseparable part of me. I was largely unaware of the appropriate vocabulary to apply to someone who had suffered a trauma. For years, even as I suffered its symptoms, I was clueless about its name. But as I learned many years later, indeed, trauma was what it was. During the years following my incarceration, I could only remember the dull ache and the all-too-frequent violent headaches that rocked my body. My body released its terrors physically where my mind could not bring itself to comprehend. The debilitating headaches became all too familiar. I knew its early signs which came just after I tensed up, my body rigid and taut, expecting something bad to happen, like the time I was with my mother at the market or when I was walking back to the dorm from school. It is not as if I have never had a headache before because I did suffer from them as a child. But the ones that I suffered from 1973 on, however, were more intense than anything I'd known previously. These were violent migraines that I battled with for long stretches of time. When it came, it was the kind of pain that would force me to lie down in a darkened room, where any bit of light or noise or movement was like a devil holding its pitchfork and ready to skewer me. If I could not darken the room sufficiently, I would close my eyes and place a pillow over my face to shield me from the light, which was like a dagger, ready to pierce straight through my skull. The throbbing, pulsating pain would intensify minute after excruciating minute. The pain in my head was the only thing I was aware of. I was my head. I had no torso, no arms, no hands, no legs, no feet, or any other body part. My tired, aching head was all that I could be. And then soon I knew an aura would come as the first flickers of tiny black dots danced around my field of vision. I braced myself for what would happen next. I would rush to the toilet in time to throw up. Once that was done, I would experience some relief. I would stumble back to bed because I would feel other parts of my body once again and these would all be tired, fatigued, and in need of rest. I would pop a headache pill into my mouth and let sleep take over. When I would awaken hours later, I would feel like I had just been run over by a truck. These headaches continued for many years and remain a part of my life even now. I slowly learned to handle them over time. But what was harder to unravel and to try to balance was the mental disequilibrium.

I went on with my life as best I could. I completed high school and entered university and armed myself with the degree that my parents expected me to earn. But even as I enjoyed some feeling of accomplishment, I was never far away from the thousand little deaths that I suffered, all of these little wounds refusing to heal. When I finally left the Philippines, and years later read Jacobo Timerman's account of his incarceration, I began to understand a little of what those little deaths meant. Reading his words from his book, *Prisoner Without a Name, Cell Without a Number*, I thought that it was me he was describing when he spoke about the terrors that struck him. For the first time, I understood the dark sentiments that had nagged at me all those years. Timerman wrote,

> *Every day, since my release, I've been waiting for some vital shock to take place, some deep extended nightmare to explode suddenly in the middle of the night, allowing me to relive it all—something that will take me back to the original scene, purify me and then restore me to this place where I am. But nothing has happened and I find this calm terrifying.*[40]

I have never grasped meaning as readily as I have at reading these words. It was as if I had written them myself. It was almost as if I could hear the first faint timbre of the bells ringing and if I would only listen a little more, the ringing would call me to where I needed to go. His words allowed me to confront my own extended nightmare, a five-year-long nightmare that lasted for even more years, long after I had stopped reporting to the camp.

---

40   Timerman, *Prisoner Without a Name, Cell Without a Number*, page 34.

Now things started to make a bit of sense. For instance, I used to puzzle over why I fantasized about what I would do in prison, should I be arrested again. Like a sword hanging over my head, I waited anxiously for the next time the soldiers would take me away; snatch me once again from the uneasy comfort of home and family. I was certain that I was going to be arrested again even if I did not do anything. These thoughts became obsessive. I endured a kind of dying by the mere question of when the military would pick me up again. I imagined that they would kidnap me the next time, most likely when I was alone so that they would not have to explain to anyone why they were taking me, and that would be the last anyone would see of me.

It was these thoughts, the 'saudade,' mixed with terrorizing fear that sprang forth from the back of my head when I read Timerman's words about the "deep extended nightmare that would explode in the middle of the night..." But at least I thought I had begun to assimilate the vocabulary I needed to understand what happened to me.

It was true that Marcos had done away with much of law and order. It was his law that mattered. So for years, I saw myself as a wounded hound dog and I fantasized about what I would do inside prison were I to be sent there again. I thought about the specific activities I would do to while away the time. I imagined myself sitting on the hard bed of my prison cell, reading the books that I had always wanted to read but never had the time for. I imagined myself writing as I leaned my back against the wall for support, using those lined yellow pads to write stories and articles. Now I would have the time and therefore, I imagined, I could summon the creativity needed to pen them.

I also fantasized about composing poems inside the prison walls, poetry being a genre of literature I had never appreciated before. But now, now I thought I could give it a chance. I began believing in and seeing the beauty of poetry and its linguistic brevity, though I was never one to be of few words. In truth, I loved to exercise the muscles of my mouth, jabbering away with friends and family, discussing or arguing points. I simply enjoyed being a chatterbox. And thus, poetry, I naively thought, might dissuade me from that verbal inclination.

In my more domestic moments of fantasy, I imagined knitting a sweater, looking like a stooped grandmother in her rocking chair; or darning socks or embroidering a piece of fabric that could be turned into a throw pillow. I could not begin to count the times that I imagined doing these activities should I be arrested again. These thoughts became a part of the internal life that I could not share with anyone. It was then that I realized that prison was no longer the camp in which I had been detained. Prison need not be the small square walls found within the highly secure grounds and fences of the camp. It had entered my head. It was there when I was in school learning algebra, science, or whatever class I was in. It was there as I went home from school, always thinking and sensing that someone was following me. It was even there when I went to Sunday mass, seeing a wrathful and vengeful God instead of a loving and compassionate deity. It was definitely there when I reported to those petty military gods every other day.

Back then I believed that these people owned me. My body was theirs to do whatever they wanted with. That was what my fifteen-year-old self believed even as I returned to school and went on to complete high school at sixteen.

That was what my seventeen-year old self believed, as I went on to university and completed an undergraduate degree by the time I turned twenty. Freedom to say the things that I wanted to say, the independence to do what I wanted to do, and the lack of fear of repercussions should I have said or did something deemed subversive—all these had now become remote possibilities. What was here and now was the endless looking over my shoulder to see if someone was following me; the constant worry that I would soon be sent to jail, tortured, and then disappeared. The realization brought with it a hundred more little deaths raining down on me.

Leaving

I n early 1979, when my graduation from university was just two months away, I decided I would leave the country at the first opportunity. I did not know how I was going to do this, but I was earnest about giving it a good try. Leaving one's homeland is difficult for many people. For others, it can be a gut-wrenching decision, particularly when leaving means going overseas, where economic opportunities abound and sooner or later the leave-taker must confront a strong disincentive to return home. Then there are those who will leave, once outside, will never be allowed to return, or should they return, will be sent to prison for being an "enemy of the state." All of these thoughts and possibilities weighed on me. The more I thought about it, the stronger was the desire to move away.

Once the decision was made, my departure could not come soon enough for me. I was tired of all the danger, real or imagined, that I lived through each day I remained in the Philippines. I wanted to be far away from the world I had known since I was born. As much as I would miss my family, I was exhausted from agonizing about what every new day meant, about safeguarding my safety as well as realizing that freedom from fear would never again be in the cards for me. I was tired of having to look over my shoulder every time I left the house. I was exhausted from the constant anxiety that nagged at me to get home as soon as dusk settled. I was tired of visiting the camp, exchanging stilted pleasantries with the guards while I dutifully signed my name in their logbook; its pages getting fuller so that a new logbook appeared with regularity every few weeks.

I was still unhappy about the state of affairs of the country. Marcos continued to rule with an iron hand. I was not alone in my desperation to get out of the country. While my reasons were not as economically motivated as these were for many Filipinos, we shared the exhaustion of living the way we did in a repressive society whose government did not give a damn. There were more and more of us who felt disenfranchised and disadvantaged; who were getting poorer by the day, and who, even with their university degrees, were unable to secure jobs. Instead of white-collar jobs, many of them chose to work as domestics in Saudi Arabia, Hong Kong, or whichever country would take them. The Filipino diaspora has started and there was no going back. Foreign remittances became a regular undertaking for those working overseas to provide for the family members they left behind.

It was almost at the day's end on a February afternoon as I wound my way from the hilly slopes of Ateneo's Loyola Heights Campus to Bellarmine Hall where the Communication Studies department was housed. I had just finished a TV production class at the university TV studios near Gate 2 of the expansive campus. I entered the building and turned towards the stairs, which I took two steps at a time to get to the third floor. I was hoping that my thesis adviser was still there. Unfortunately, he had already left, the department secretary, C., informed me. She then handed me an envelope.

"Here's something for you that came in the mail today," she said.

"What is it?" I asked.

"Open it," she replied.

The label on the envelope told me that the letter was from overseas. The return address read: Communications Institute, East West Center in Hawaii. Two months earlier, I had applied for a research fellowship with the institute. I whizzed through the contents as fast as I could hoping to find what I was looking for. As soon as I did, I jumped up and down, clutching the paper close to my chest and giving C. a big smile. I hugged her and said,

"Oh my god, you won't believe it. Guess what, I won the research fellowship I applied for. Gee whiz, now I know what I will be doing after graduation, isn't that neat? And it will be in Hawaii. Oh my gosh!"

She hugged me back and said, "I am happy for you. It will be an honor for the department that you won the award. I will tell our chairman to make an announcement about it."

"Thanks. They want me to be there by April," I replied.

The truth is, I did not think I was going to get the fellowship. I was told that I might not get it because I was still an undergrad student when I had applied and most fellowships were awarded to graduate students. I could not have been happier. When I decided months earlier that I was going to leave the country, I had actively looked for ways out. This was one of them. With the letter in my hand, I felt a relief that I had not felt in a long time. The country that had jailed me had no place in my nineteen-year-old heart. I was pleased to go and hopefully take my miseries with me, dropping them, if only psychologically, into the swells of the Pacific Ocean as I made my way on a plane bound for Honolulu. If only for a while, I reasoned, I would not have to think about being picked up again, arrested when I least expected it, or fearful that the next time around I would not be so lucky.

I woke up much earlier than usual on the day I left the Philippines for the first time. I had been too excited to sleep the night before. I woke up early and got myself dressed with plenty of time to spare. Not having anything else to do, I folded the pleats of my batik-inspired printed skirt carefully, even though these were not creased. I adjusted the straps of the sleeveless top of the same fabric. I was wearing an outfit of muted browns, white, and beige cotton fabric; one that I had chosen especially for the occasion. I thought it was stylish enough even if I was not much into fashion. I also wanted it to have an ethnic flair about it. I walked again, the third time I think, towards the mirror attached to the door of the armoire in my bedroom to have another look. It was a very hot day. I was glad I chose this summer dress. I'd be comfortable in it, I thought, only to realize later once airborne that the plane's air conditioning would be blasting away during the long ten-hour flight to the other end of the Pacific, and I was chilly throughout the flight.

I glanced down towards my suitcase on the floor. I opened it and surveyed its contents, making sure I had everything I needed. I opened my purse for the nth time to check my passport, plane ticket, and my American dollars. Then I walked downstairs, suitcase in hand. Tatang saw me as I was descending the stairs. He immediately got up from where he was seated by the dining table, the place where he usually sorted through his mail and papers related to his trucking business.

"Let your brother carry that," he said. "It is too heavy for you." He looked towards my brother, K.

"Take the luggage from your sister; it's too heavy for her," he ordered my brother. "And by the way, you are coming with us," he continued talking to him in Kapampangan.

K. pranced up the short, varnished steps and took the suitcase from me. He took it to the car where Tang's driver, Ely, was fiddling with the engine, checking things out.

"Are you ready?" Tang asked me. He was dressed in casual dark-colored slacks, a striped golf shirt, and shiny black leather shoes. Taking out his comb from his back trouser pocket, he slid its fine teeth through his hair. Tatang has always been fastidious about his appearance. Then, he announced,

"*Tara, mako tana. Maranon pa pero pota matrapic tamu.*" (Lets' go. We'd better leave now. It is still quite early but we might get caught in traffic otherwise.)

As soon as he said this, part of me wanted to stay, even though I was really excited to leave. Looking at my watch, I found that we had roughly six and a half hours before my flight. Knowing father, who knew Manila traffic well, having commuted between Manila and San Fernando for years, he would definitely want us to leave early. Besides, he was just that kind of guy, who was never late for anything. Anyway, I was too fidgety myself at this time to worry about it; I too wanted us to be early in arriving at the airport.

The drive should take us about two hours but with all the traffic, it would probably take us about three and a half hours. I'd still have about three hours before my first international flight, which would stop over in Tokyo and then fly on to Honolulu, arriving there early in the morning. Tatang tried to lighten up the growing tension in the car by making conversation about this or that. I could tell that he was nervous too. Maybe he was worried about his nineteen-year-old daughter taking her first trip overseas, I reasoned. Fair enough. I certainly would be too.

America seemed like such a far-away place. It was a place we had conjured in our minds as the 'land of milk and honey' though we were also exposed to the excesses in its culture particularly on drugs and other things that we saw on TV. In the view of conservative Filipino parents, it was a place where bad things could happen to their children. I was thinking these thoughts and trying to come up with ways to tell Tatang not to worry about me. I even thought to say, "Tang, don't you worry. I won't go to parties, will not talk to men who are strangers, etc., etc." But then I told myself, maybe I shouldn't or he'd just worry more. So I kept quiet in the back seat. Instead, I took out the rosary from my purse. Grandma had given it to me a few days ago as a parting gift. She specifically said it was blessed by our parish priest, and was sure it would protect me from all harm. My deeply, deeply Catholic family, I thought. I loved them, but this whole talk about religion could sometimes be pretty stifling. I thanked her graciously, and said I would always remember her when I used the rosary. Besides, I told Grandma, it is not as if I will not be back.

We made it to the airport, just as I predicted, with plenty of time to spare. Tang appeared nervous as we got out of the car and he was helping me carry my luggage towards the check-in entrance. Seeing his worried look, I said, in a happier tone than I truly felt, "Tang, don't worry. Everything's going to be alright."

I didn't want to tell him what was really bothering me. Despite my excitement about the opportunity to go abroad, there was a strong fear gripping me at that moment, particularly as we saw the machine-gun toting guards at the airport's entrance. I was afraid that when they saw my name, they would not allow me to leave the country. We had heard about Filipinos prohibited from leaving, as the government wanted to keep an eye on them, as we were still under martial law at the time. My heart was pounding by the time I lined up at the Philippine Airlines check-in counter. I felt uneasy that at any minute, a soldier would grab me roughly and say, "No, ma'am, you're not allowed to board that plane." Tang and my brother, K., were standing next to me while I was waiting for my turn at the check-in counter, making light conversation.

Little did I know that the fear I had was also my father's. Many years later, my sister, C. intimated how nervous Tang was about that trip to the airport. He was so worried that I would not be allowed to leave the country. He told her that only after I was able to check in without any incident and proceeded to the gate and said goodbye did he feel relief. He said that as much as he did not want me to go to a foreign land by myself, he was also glad that I was out of the Philippines because, like me, he worried constantly about my safety.

As I sat in the window seat for the flight to Tokyo, my anxiety continued. I clutched the rosary tightly in my hand. I did not want the chains attaching the beads to break so I loosened my grip. My palms had become sweaty. Finally, the pilot announced that we were ready to take off. This is it. Several minutes later, as we reached cruising altitude and the land below faded, and all I could see from my airplane seat as I looked out were clouds, I breathed a heavy sigh. I was safe. I had made it out. Ten hours later, the plane touched down at the Honolulu International Airport.

Disembarking from the plane, I looked around me, the morning sun ablaze over the hills; skies clear, blue and dotted with white like huge cotton balls. I felt the urge to kiss the ground but for the fact that I did not want strange looks sent my way from fellow passengers. As I walked down the tarmac, the iconic Hawaiian palms I have seen in many pictures swayed in the light breeze. As a bus picked us up at the tarmac to take us to the terminal, I still could not believe I was here. On that pleasant April morning in 1979 at the Honolulu airport, I experienced the most happiness I had genuinely felt in years since I was fifteen. It was a feeling I will never forget.

A few days later, as the workshops at Burns Hall winded down for the day and I was walking down East-West Center Road with the university on one side and the East-West Center on the other, the serene Japanese garden next to Jefferson Hall beckoned me to sit and watch the koi in the pond. I plopped down on the soft green grass and watch the sun's afternoon rays speckled the trees' foliage. I enjoyed the silence the garden brought and felt lighter, as if a burden had been lifted. I was floating once again, but this time, conscious of the bliss I felt, and not because my mind shut itself off to ward away horror. Later, I learned to take this memory out and relive it in times when I was reeling from the destruction wrought by the ugly re-emerging heads of my personal monsters.

The Personal and the Political

I returned to the Philippines after I completed my fellowship at the East-West Center. The fellowship was part of a scholarship and cultural exchange program and the U.S. Government issued special category visas called J-1 to foreign scholars in these exchanges, which required them to return to their home country once the fellowship expires. Before leaving the U.S., I explored opportunities to consider graduate school as I discovered that I was beginning to enjoy the institutional culture of academic research found in America.

Back in Manila, I went about applying to graduate school to American institutions. In between, I secured a job working at a research and consulting outfit and on evenings and weekends, I taught undergraduate courses at a local university. As if these were not enough, I enrolled in a couple of graduate courses at the University of the Philippines. I surmised that I needed to calm the tempest roaring inside me and the distractions were useful in my not paying attention to it. Yet, I was not entirely successful in warding it off.

One day, I was sitting on a bench under an acacia tree next to a government building, eating lunch with my

American friend, J., who was in Manila doing field study for his doctoral degree. As we ate our sandwiches, the tree's pink blossoms fell down on us. Then we started talking about career plans after graduate school. I told him that I was waiting to hear about my applications to graduate school scholarships in the U.S. I also told him that if I failed to be awarded a scholarship, it would be okay and that it did not really matter.

"Why," he asked curiously.

He insisted that I deserved to get it, that I work hard and have good, solid academic credentials. Then he saw how sad I became.

"What's wrong?" he asked.

"I don't know," I began. At first I was reluctant to tell him more. But after prodding me further, I told him, "Maybe because I don't think I am going to live long."

"Jesus! Why do you say that?" He looked at me with a total lack of understanding like I was insane.

"I can't believe what I am hearing from you. Gosh, you are young, smart, pretty, and the world is ready for the likes of you. Why the hell would you say or worse, think that you are going to die soon," he asked, seemingly angry with me. "Are you sick?" he asked.

"No, not as far as I know," I replied.

"Then why?" he continued.

"I don't know. I just do. I feel it," I replied and left it at that.

The thoughts of death at that time in my life were persistent. It was understandable to me but not fully comprehensible. I didn't expect that the thought of dying young would cling to me for so long; it impressed me that it was occupying every nook and cranny of my brain.

It was Kumander Dante, who once said,

Freedom from prison is temporary and senseless as long as we continuously live under a shadow of fear and anxiety.

He understood. He lived it too. Everyone who has ever experienced the terror of political incarceration knows. Some time ago, I was reading something C.S. Lewis wrote which offered me some understanding on the fear and anxiety that have permanently domiciled within me. He said,

It is easy to say you believe a rope to be strong and sound as long as you are using it to cord a box. But suppose you had to hang by that rope over a precipice. Wouldn't you discover how much you really trusted it? [41]

At that stage in my life, the political detention I suffered had come down to a basic choice: life or death. If I chose life, it was one that was controlled by those who enslaved me. If I chose death, then I have given up. I could not detect any shade of gray in a life led under such constant surveillance. Even as I myself did not suffer physical torture, the uncertainty of not knowing whether I was going to experience just that at some point was enough to put me in a tangled web of psychological maladies.

Then I asked myself, how much do I trust Marcos and his men to do the right thing? How much did I really trust them not to send me back into detention? Not much was my answer.

---

41   Taken from C.S. Lewis' book, *A Grief Observed*, first published in England by Faber and Faber Limited in 1961. It was reissued with a foreword by Madeline L'Engle in 1989 by HarperCollins Publishers.

For a moment, let us suppose that Marcos' supporters
and critics of the left would claim that Marcos was truly
a great leader. They would further argue that it was the
left who was responsible for the mayhem and violence in
the 1970s. Let's also suppose that the foreign media and
scholars did not write about the atrocities committed under
martial law, a period described by one local journalist as
"marked by incredible carnage."[42] Finally, let's suppose that
Amnesty International did not investigate or report on the
atrocities perpetuated by both sides.

For a fifteen-year-old girl, do these suppositions render
her story untrue? Were the fear, the anxiety, and the
constant threat of danger and safety all imagined? Why
would she suffer so much when countless others had
endured far worst? These are the questions I asked myself
over and over again. Their possible answers would affect me
like a contagious disease. It didn't matter if I was a student,
a worker, a wife, or a mother, or whether I was living in the
Philippines, or even when I left to live in the United States.
It haunted me for decades, not knowingly on my part, but
nevertheless, I was always aware of its presence. Not until
I reached my forties did this painful odyssey end, and only
because an illness finally paved a way out.

Despite the credible evidence and extensive stories of
abuse during martial law told by historians, scholars, as
well as its victims, I believe that there will be those in the
Philippines who will willfully maintain that this dreadful
political chapter never happened. They will be zealous in
this belief because they saw Marcos as a good man and
one who could not have committed such brutality (though

42   As described by Amando Doronila in "*Analysis: Politics of Violence*," Philippine
Inquirer column found online at http://opinion.inquirer.net/inquireropinion/columns/
view/20070824-84405/Politics_of_violence, August 24, 2007.

there were enough bloody corpses, had they cared to look) and blatant disregard for civil society. They are entitled to this belief.

But so are those whose view of Marcos and his administration is one in which corruption, abuse of power, disregard for poverty, and entrenched cronyism weakened the country. They too are entitled to think this way. The two opposing sides are coupled, not in solidarity, but in *mano a mano* moves designed to repel one another. Moves, whose victims are ordinary civilians; they are those who have suffered and whose lives have not improved.

Marcos is long gone and Imelda's attempts to rewrite history have become muted over the years. But the dirty ways of politics have stayed and remain entrenched in president after president post-Marcos. Filipinos I have spoken to about these issues go even further in saying that the political waters, if anything, have gotten more muddied. While the country's neighbors have taken advantage of the so-called 'Asian century' to lift their peoples out of poverty and generally improve their lot, the Philippines continues to lag behind.

As I relegated the political twists and turns of the country to the background when I left for America, time and again, I found myself having to deal with the unexpected consequences of incarceration, or more precisely, the trauma, which seemed to dog me when I least expected it. There is no doubt in my mind that its pernicious effects had taken up permanent residence in my psyche until I learned to deal with them.

After I was released, I did not know how long I was going to live under such uncertainty and it left me with a defeated spirit. How could it not? The devices employed by Marcos' rule under martial law rarely stopped rapping at my door. Regularly making my presence known at the camp demarcated the physical and social spaces I inhabited. Each visit to the camp guaranteed the success of these devices in breaking one's spirit. Then there were the boundaries I imposed upon myself—where I should not go, who I should not associate with, why I must ignore my desire to write, why I must reject a career as a lawyer, a journalist or a writer—all intended to keep me away from trouble.

Is it any wonder then that my spirit felt shattered in more ways than I could count? Or, perhaps, I was the type who was susceptible to having her spirit weakened, despite the absence of the physical horror and the brutal treatment of the body. As I look back at it now, I am sad at the mere contemplation about what my spirit could have been like had I not experienced what I did. My heart feels heavy at the thought that I experienced it when I was so young and vulnerable. It was an age I understood to be a transition— the completion of my years as a little girl and on the cusp of discovering the many and varied pathways to adulthood. Instead, this transition screeched to a grounding halt because I had become solely focused on staying alive, or at least, in keeping myself away from prison walls.

After 1973, I began to believe that it was wrong for me to feel the way I did because I had only suffered psychological wounds, whereas thousands of Filipinos endured both the physical and psychological wounds inflicted by the brutal trial of martial law. I convinced myself that it was wrong for me to suffer as much as they did because, after all, I was fortunate enough to make it home that Christmas, while others languished behind bars for years.

I did not fully understand the debilitating effect the camp ritual had on me until years later. Its effect was not on my radar until illness revealed it. In January 2004, I was diagnosed with thyroid cancer. After the surgery, and while commencing cancer treatment, I saw my cancer doctor every four weeks for a period of almost two years.

Before every visit to his office, I had to convince myself that I was going to be okay, but still, I was anxious, and many times, panicked. My body found a way to deal with what was bottled up inside. My body shook; the shaking was distressing, not to mention, embarrassing. If I was walking, I needed to sit down, if only to press my hands against my thighs to keep them from shaking so hard that I looked epileptic. My heart beat wildly inside my chest. I took to carrying a small hand towel or a handkerchief with me wherever I went in order to wipe my abnormally sweaty palms. At the back of my mind, I sensed these physical manifestations were not unfamiliar to me, though I was too focused on the cancer at the time to give them serious contemplation.

Also, I was once again preoccupied with dying, and with it, the thought of leaving my two young sons behind. I believed then that I would suffer a similar fate as my mother, who died of cancer when she was forty-four years old, leaving behind many young children, the youngest of which was only four. My mother died only two years after I had been released from prison. So the panic and anxiety disorder that my doctor diagnosed, I mistakenly thought were simply manifestations of my worry about the disease and the untimely death of my mother. My doctor also complained that my blood pressure was always high. I had not been prone to hypertension until then. I prided myself in being healthy except for the migraines that I regularly suffered. I watched my diet and exercise was a regular part of my routine.

In the first few months after the cancer diagnosis, I was simply unable to overcome the debilitating panic, despite my doctor's confidence that the thyroid cancer was, as he put it, "not only treatable but curable." The surgeon who operated on me, who I not only admired for her dexterity at surgery, but also for her compassion and understanding as a human being (she insisted on visiting me at the nuclear medicine unit while I was radioactive), said the same thing. She even claimed, "If I had a choice of a cancer, this is the one I would choose. Perhaps, I would even prefer it over an extreme case of diabetes." The endocrinologist who administered my treatment at the nuclear medicine unit of the hospital also said as much. He said, "The treatment is almost an afterthought, or anti-climactic if you will, when you compare it to the seven or so weeks you underwent on a low-iodine diet, waiting for your body to be starved of iodine after which you were fatigued and suffered from headaches and all that." There was no reason to doubt him. He was a well-respected thyroid specialist who was asked his expert opinion about Supreme Court Chief Justice William Rehnquist's thyroid cancer by *The Washington Post*.

Yet, my brain stubbornly refused to believe any of them. It was not that I did not trust them. But my persistent, on-edge psychological state drowned out all rationality. Any lucidity I once possessed was now hopelessly obscured. It came to a point when having my monthly medical check-ups were so nerve-wracking that I disallowed the nurse from closing the door in the windowless examination room, due to my claustrophobia.

My doctor offered to put me in touch with another cancer specialist upon seeing my deepening anxious state. In his opinion, if he was the source of my anxiety, we could remedy it by me going to another doctor. He added that he wouldn't be offended. I refused. He had come highly recommended by my family physician, someone I trusted and felt confident in all medical matters. Still, I labored. The visits felt like I was waiting for a death sentence. The check-ups revolved around palpating my neck and then taking blood samples and the ensuing lab work that would reveal the results of the cancer marker. After each visit, more anxious waiting followed. A week would pass before the clinic would call me to say if the test was fine or not. In between, I agonized over the thought that this might be the time when they would tell me that the cancer was back. When I looked in the mirror, I could not recognize the person I had become. My face seemed frightened most of the time. It was gaunt, pale, and gray. I had lost weight. I had no interest in eating, I never felt hungry. But my doctor warned that I must eat. So, I forced myself even when food was stuck in my throat and refused to go down.

Then, one day, in a very desperate moment, that little voice of long ago came back. It told me to seek help and not to give up. Help came during a particularly exhausting day. I was waiting for the overdue result of the thyrogen test. I was beside myself, not knowing whether to call the clinic or to wait until they called me. It was an excruciating period of waiting. On top of this, the therapist I had been seeing was out of town but left word that another therapist was covering for her, if I needed one. I did. The substitute therapist asked me a series of questions and then after some thought, asked me if I would consider hypnotherapy. She briefly explained what it entailed. I then told her, with all the conviction I could muster, that I was willing to try anything. I felt helpless and desperate; but nonetheless, something inside me felt it was time to replace the fear and anxiety with sanity and humanity. She then gave me the name of a hypnotherapist. I called him as soon as I hung up the phone. I saw him for the next few weeks, with each session being recorded so that I could listen to it as many times as I wanted. It gave me some relief but not enough. He did tell me that I also needed to see a regular therapist, which I did. I saw her at the same time I was going through cancer treatment.

Several months after I began seeing her, I was talking about my past and of my childhood one day, when something alerted her to what I just said. All of a sudden, she looked at me intently and then said,

"Excuse me, but did you just tell me that you were sent to prison as a political prisoner when you were fifteen?"

"Yes?" I said quizzically raising my eyebrow, wondering if I had said something wrong.

"And then you followed that with your saying that you had to report to the military camp every other day and then every two weeks, or something like that for five years?" she continued to ask.

"Yes," I said again, puzzled at the way she was repeating what I told her.

"And now, you see your cancer doctor every four weeks, and each time you do, you become very anxious, and all that?" she further said.

"Yes," I repeated. She must be on to something here.

"Let's stop right here, if we may," she said. "I would like you to see a psychiatrist I work with on a regular basis. I want you to reconsider your decision not to take medication for your anxiety and panic. I think that you really need something to help you right now. I want you to see him and with your permission, I would like to discuss your case with him. I now have a good idea about what is happening to you, but I would like you to see him first and then we can all confer."

She proceeded to give me his name and encouraged me to book an appointment as soon as possible. I did so. At the appointed hour, I was my increasingly nervous self as I waited for the psychiatrist. His office, on a leafy street in the Chevy Chase suburb of Maryland, was a pleasant and light-filled room decorated with warm colors that were meant to calm and to soothe. The doctor asked me to confirm what my therapist had shared with him. After I did, he explained in a tone suffused with an equal dose of thoughtfulness and compassion, that what I was suffering from is called 'delayed post-traumatic stress disorder.' He said that the monthly visits to my doctor to monitor the cancer marker had triggered the original trauma I had suffered. That trauma, he explained, was my arrest at fifteen combined with the weekly reporting to the military camp for years. He recommended that I take a low-dose anti-anxiety medication to help me cope with my cancer doctor visits as well as hashing through the trauma issues in regular psychotherapy sessions. I had resisted any kind of medication up to this point. I was convinced that I was already getting my fair share of medicine with the cancer treatment; I did not need to pump my body with more.

After an initial reluctance, I found myself agreeing as the doctor explained his reasoning. I was exhausted from the intense feelings I have at every waking moment. His gentle demeanor, plus the soft and kind voice he had when talking, indicated that he was committed to helping me.

From that point on, I began my journey towards understanding the effects my incarceration had on me and of trying to rebuild what had been destroyed. Incarceration, to me was like a stubborn, crusty mud, staining one's black rubber boots. You need a hose to spray the mud off and as you do, you will begin to see the hardened mud soften and then turn into dark brown water sloshing off the boots; and soon the dirt is washed off completely, though it will take time to experience that refreshing sight of clean footwear that you are only too willing to put back on your feet. I must have needed loads and loads of water to wash off the hardened pain and social vilification. It was a torturous journey in merely figuring out what was wrong.

I knew I was finally free of it when I was able to go back to the scene of the crime on a trip back to the Philippines. My therapist and I had worked very hard to reach that point. The 'aha' moment came when I began thinking that I was tired of being in favor of the "against," and was ready to be in favor of "for." Not against myself but for myself. Not against those who sent me to prison but rather for understanding what made them do it.

My recovery was slow. But one of the things I found as I went through it was something about grief and trauma best expressed by someone who had lived it. This voice comes from the mother of one of the victims aboard an airplane that was bombed and crashed over Lockerbie, Scotland in 1988. Her name is Suse Lowenstein. Her words became a salve to the slow healing of my wounds. When asked about the grief she suffered, she said,

"I happen to be a great believer in denial. You can't do it all at once. It's just too much."[43]

Yes, I agree that it was way too much. There were many times when I could not take it all. The process of healing felt like tiny trickles of water dripping from a leaky faucet.

---

43   Suse Lowenstein said this in talking to authors, Ron Marasco and Brian Shuff, as found in their book, *About Grief: Insights, Setbacks, Grace Notes, Taboo.* (Chicago: Ivan R. Dee Publishers, 2010), page 73.

My mind only divulged what I was ready for, never rushing me when I was not ready, even when I was anxious to get it over quickly. It is what happened in the writing of this book. Writing has taken a long time and there were times when I could not touch it for weeks, and sometimes for months, because it was too much. My mind and my spirit were simply not ready.

When trauma and its effects take up residence, it is a formidable task to unseat them. At its most vicious, trauma hovers around like a reckless assassin, ready to pounce. One takes cover whenever and however one can, until out of frustration, the assassin leaves. As I went through each hiding, I was inexplicably aided by that tiny voice, the one who often spoke to me during the most painful and desperate periods of my life. Some would say this voice was my conscience. Others said it was something else. Whatever it is, I simply call it the voice. When a jolt appears, I waited for the voice to speak. I listened. I learned that despite my desperation, I could be called upon to do something and do it well.

One unforgettable moment when that voice spoke happened in a conversation I once had with my then fifteen-year-old-son. I had just picked him up from his school, one cold winter evening, after he finished his driver education class. As was usual, I asked him how his day went. I knew there was something on his mind as soon as he quickly told me his day was fine.

"Listen, mom," he began. "There were college representatives visiting our school today. Also, a military recruiter was there. He said that there is going to be an information meeting on military recruitment in a few days. I am thinking of attending it."

As soon as I heard what he said, I angrily said,

"Don't tell me you are attending. Really, what are you thinking? Join the military? Really? Why would you want to do that?"

"I did not say I was going to join the military. I was just going to attend the meeting and find out what it is about."

"Even then," I insisted. "Why would you even consider doing that?"

My son grew quiet and I could see he was hurt by what I just told him. But despite this, my anger persisted. At the same time, I was ashamed about how I behaved. Once I sufficiently calmed down, I apologized to him for being so unreasonable. Like the soft-hearted and loving young man that he is, he accepted my apology though I could tell I hurt his feelings just because of the uncalled for intense opposition that I displayed for something he considered to be so harmless and trivial.

Later that night, I found sleep elusive. I got up and went downstairs and began thinking about the conversation I had with my son. It then dawned on me why I reacted so negatively. Here, he was at fifteen years old, taking an interest in the military, though not seriously as he told me, yet I could not separate this from what I, as a fifteen year old, has suffered under the Philippine military. I did not even have the sensibility to distinguish between the U.S. military and the one that inflicted my suffering in the Philippines. I became alarmed at the thought. I then decided that I was going to do whatever it took to change things for me as well as for my son, who I have unintentionally hurt because of my own demons. This realization to change things and the journey towards doing so, in time, became a pleasant discovery.

Grace Notes

There is a vitality, a life force, a quickening that is translated through you into action, and because there is only one of you in all time, the expression is unique. And if you block it, it will never exist through any other medium… And be lost. The world will not have it.

- Martha Graham

It was a sunny and pleasant summer day. I, my husband and our two sons were at the house we rented for our annual holiday in the Catskill Mountains in rural New York. The Catskills played a big part in my husband's boyhood summer experience, and, we continued the tradition with our young children in spending part of our summers there. The trip was made more special this time as two of my sisters were able to join us; my older sister, Cynthia, who had flown in all the way from the Philippines, and Timmee, who often joined us, taking the bus from New York City. I was thrilled to show my older sister, Cynthia, this beautiful part of America that held so many pleasant memories for my husband, our two boys, and me.

The house we rented was right next to a bridge over the Delaware River. From there, one could view the green expanse of trees dotting the river's shores as well as spot the occasional bald eagle, which would be signaled by its distant cry. We had just finished kayaking on the river and also had done a bit of fishing. When we got tired and hungry, we went back to the house.

My sisters and I sat down around the table that was nestled by the kitchen's bay window, a place where we could look out over the trees and the river. Cynthia had brought some goodies from the Philippines; dried and salted watermelon seeds and dry roasted corn nuts, seasoned with lots of crunchy garlic. As we ate the seeds, corn nuts and other snacks we had brought from home in the Washington, DC suburb, the three of us began telling stories, particularly those we remembered from our childhoods.

"Do you remember when we would sneak out of the house and walk through the rice fields, and we would get muddy all the way up to our knees?" Timmee asked.

"Oh, yes, I remember," I replied. "I was so scared that we were walking so far away from home, thinking that we would get lost. Or that Tatang would really get mad at us for doing things that we were not supposed to."

Cynthia looked at us, hardly believing what she was hearing.

"When did you guys run away like that?" she asked.

"All the time," Timmee said.

"But especially during the rainy season when we could hear the frogs, oh my god, they were so loud, they kept us awake at night. But when we heard the frogs singing, we knew that there would be lots of tadpoles in those muddy rice paddies."

"Yes, that would be why we went there, wouldn't it?" I added. "We were always trying to catch those tadpoles and those little fishes with our bare hands, while we tramped in the mud, and then wondered afterwards how we could sneak back into the house without Tatang or the adults seeing us, covered with mud and our clothes all dirty. But then we would quickly walk past the house and head for Juliet's house, where we washed up since her mother did not mind what we did."

Cynthia continued to look bewildered. She considered herself to be the big sister, the babysitter to all of us, and had a hard time accepting that we kept sneaking out of the house and going to forbidden places without her knowledge.

"Wow, I was supposed to take care of you guys. Where was I?" she asked. She had always been the type to take care of people and still does. Maybe that is why she became a doctor. She prided herself in doing her job well at all times and as children, she took seriously her task of taking care of us when our parents were away.

It was then that we talked about how, despite our having fun and wandering through those fields, we also knew that we were courting trouble especially if we stayed there as dusk approached. We discussed how scary those times sometimes were. Then out of the blue, I thought of asking my older sister what she remembered of the events that happened in 1973. I did not know why, but at just that moment, I felt the time was finally right to ask her what she thought, what she experienced, and more importantly what she knew about my parents' reactions about the whole thing.

"So, tell me," I began. "I never heard from Ima and Tang what they really thought about what happened to me. We never talked about it. The only reference I remember from the two of them about it was that they would remind me to report to the camp so that I would not be in further trouble with the military."

My mother had died barely two years after I was detained. Tatang died in his eighties in 2005.

"What was it like for them when they found out that the soldiers picked me up at school? How did they take it?" I continued. Instead of answering me directly, she said,

"The day I found out you were sent to military camp, the first thought I had was why her? Why not me? I honestly thought what a great honor it would have been to be arrested, to be sent to jail for one's beliefs, for pushing the envelope, so to speak, against injustice, corruption, malfeasance, and raging against the rot that the whole country was mired in. I was honestly envious that you managed to get yourself arrested and I didn't. Perhaps, this does not make sense to you because why would anyone want to be arrested? But I believe then and still do that it was a badge of honor. An honor to oppose Marcos' dictatorial hold on the Philippines."

As she said these words, her voice began to crack.

"But then, of course, I also had to think about what it was like for you. How were you treated there? You were only fifteen and what did you know? Why did the school principal allow the soldiers to take you away? When I thought about this, I became really angry. Then I spoke to Ima and Tang when I got home that day. Tang was very, very upset with Ms. Arceo. He was cursing at her, wondering why the hell she allowed the soldiers to take away her fifteen-year-old daughter, particularly from the supposedly safe haven of the Benedictine convent school. Where were the nuns, those fierce, disciplined German nuns who founded the school and who should have been there facing the soldiers. He was very angry, but then he also told me how so very proud he was of you. He was proud that you stood for your principles. He said this fully knowing that someone might hear him and that he could get in trouble. He said he was in a difficult position due to his career as a civil servant but that he wanted us to know that he did not agree with what Marcos was doing to the country and its people."

I started to cry but I managed to ask,

"What about Ma?"

"Ma was just as proud of you," she answered.

Hearing this, I could not stop the tears and my two sisters started crying too.

Then I said, "I was wrong then to think what I thought all these years that they were ashamed of me, too ashamed to even talk about it. If I had just one wish, just now, as we sit around here, I would wish that Ima and Tatang could be sitting right here with us and I was fifteen again and could hear them saying the words that you just said."

But my parents are now gone and these words will never be uttered. I cannot blame them, nor have I ever blamed them. What I know is that they suffered too. I also know enough to understand that my parents belonged to a generation where these things did not come easily. Emotional sentiments were not talked about; Filipinos were not equipped to talk candidly about feelings in the way Americans tend to do. It is not considered proper to let 'your guts hang out.' This lack of a language for communicating feelings typified my parents' generation.

But it did not matter, I silently resolved. It was very brave of them to tell Cynthia. It was courageous of them to admit that they did not like Marcos and his government. I also resolved that it was okay to know that they were proud of me and to have known this through my sister rather than hear it directly from them. It was enough to know. While hearing it from them directly would have been the best and indeed heaven sent, there is nothing wrong with second best.

NOTES AND SOURCES

Much of what has been written in these pages depended on the recollections and flashes of memory gleaned over some thirty years. While the story is my own, I have relied on historical accounts in other publications to confirm what I myself had witnessed during the Marcos years. And even though I write in English, I believe that the story could only be truly enhanced by my recollections of conversations and thoughts experienced in my own language. There are times, such as this storytelling, when I won't deny my tribal inclinations: I am a Kapampangan first. To think about specific incidents and details in my language helped me relive what was painful. That was why it was important to quote the remembered conversations, the terms of endearment and other words in Kapampangan. More important, it provided me with a rich canvas to draw from in telling my story, which for many years I buried. Not anymore.

In addition to the footnotes found in this book, I have relied on the following publications in helping me remember and understand political events in the Philippines in the 1970s.

Abinales, P., (1998). *State leaders, apparatuses and local strongmen: the Philippine military under Marcos.* In P. N. Abinales. *Images of state power: essays on Philippine politics from the margins,* (pp.100-136). Quezon City: University of the Philippines Press.

Brillantes, G., (2005). Chronicles of interesting times: essays, discourses, gems of wisdom, some laughs and other non-biodegradable articles. Pasig City: Anvil Publishing.

Chapman, W., (1987). *Inside the Philippine revolution: the new people's army and its struggles for power.* New York, NY: W.W. Norton & Company.

Karnow, S., (1989). *In our image: America's empire in the Philippines.* New York: Ballantine Books.

Marasco, R., and Shuff, B., (2010). *About grief: insights, setbacks, grace notes, taboos.* Chicago, IL: Ivan R. Dee Publishers.

McDougald, C., (1993). *Asian loot: unearthing the secrets of Marcos, Yamashita and the gold.* San Francisco: San Francisco Publishers.

Partnoy, A., (1986). *The little school: tales of disappearance and survival.* San Francisco, CA: Cleiss Press.

Pimentel, B., (1991). *Rebolusyon: a generation of struggle in the Philippines.* New York, NY: Monthly Review Press.

Rainer, T., (1998). *Your life as story: discovering the "new autobiography" and writing memoir as literature.* New York, NY: Jeremy P. Tarcher/ Putnam.

Rosenberg, D., (1979). *Marcos and martial law in the Philippines.* Ithaca, NY: Cornell University Press.

Seagrave, S., (1988). *The Marcos dynasty.* New York, NY: Ballantine Books.

Scheffler, J., (ed.), (2002). *Wall tappings; an international anthology of women's prison writings 200 to the present.* New York, NY: The Feminist Press at the City University of New York.

TFDP, (1986). *Pumipiglas: political detention and military atrocities in the Philippines 1981-1982.* Quezon City: TFDP Association of Major Religious Superiors in the Philippines.

Tuazon, B., (ed.), (1993). *Pumipiglas 3: torment and struggle after Marcos.* Quezon City: TFDP.

Timerman, J., (1988). *Prisoner without a name, cell without a number.* New York, NY: Vintage Books Edition.

Todorov, T., (2009). *Torture and the war on terror.* London: Seagull Books.

www.ingramcontent.com/pod-product-compliance
Lightning Source LLC
Chambersburg PA
CBHW072132270326
41931CB00010B/1741